WHAT A YEAR IT WAS!

1964

A walk back in time to revisit
what life was like in the year that
has special meaning for you...

*Congratulations
and
Best Wishes*

To

From

DEDICATION

To My Daughter, Laurie Cohn Rosenthal

*The most wonderful event of 1964 was your birth. Into the world you came,
this gentle, kind, loving, beautiful, talented, spiritual soul who would
grow into the daughter, wife and parent that every mother dreams
of but only a few are lucky enough to actually have.*

*Thank you for all your love and support over the years and as we
complete our 20th book together, thank you for helping make the
WHAT IT YEAR IT WAS! series so very successful.*

*Love,
Mom*

Series Created By • Beverly Cohn
Designers • Peter Hess & Marguerite Jones
Research • Laurie Cohn Rosenthal

Special thanks to Kenny Bookbinder for his invaluable help with the Sports section.

CONTENTS

POLITICS  1964
&WORLD EVENTS

DEMOCRATS SUPPORT LYNDON JOHNSON FOR THE PRESIDENCY

Mr. Johnson was thrust into office following the assassination of President Kennedy in Dallas and now he seeks to become president in his own right.

He is opposed by Republican **Barry Goldwater** in a hot and heavy political campaign.

When the votes are counted, President Johnson has a plurality of 16 million and a landslide vote returns him to office with **Hubert Humphrey** as his vice president.

1964

CIVIL RIGHTS ACT IS PASSED

At long last, Abraham Lincoln's dream of equality comes to fruition.

At the White House, on this historic occasion, **President Johnson** signs the Civil Rights Act into law just a few hours after the House approves the measure. Before a distinguished audience of legislators and civil rights leaders, President Johnson affixes his signature, using more than a hundred pens.

One of the coveted souvenirs goes to the Nobel Prize winner **Martin Luther King Jr.**, a dedicated leader of his race.

" *We must not approach the observance and enforcement of this law in a vengeful spirit. Its purpose is not to punish. Its purpose is not to divide but to end divisions, divisions which have lasted all too long. Its purpose is national, not regional. This Civil Rights Act is a challenge to all of us, to go to work in our communities and our states, in our homes and in our hearts, to eliminate the last vestiges of injustice in our beloved country.* "

WHAT A YEAR IT WAS!

GEORGE WALLACE, segregationist governor of Alabama, withdraws his independent candidacy for president.

Senator BARRY GOLDWATER is nominated for president of the U.S. at the 28th Republican national convention.

Investigating the assassination of President Kennedy, the Warren Commission issues a report calling for a sweeping revision of the Secret Service and recommends that the killing of a president or vice president be made a federal crime.

PRESIDENT JOHNSON ADDRESSES THE U.S. CHAMBER OF COMMERCE IN WASHINGTON

President Johnson optimistically predicts that business profits will be up several billion to $30 billion this year. He comments on several current events:

"...and I said to Secretary McNamara last night at dinner, 'Please get some of your top colonels and generals out of Tonkin and these other countries so they can buy things in the way of equipment from us so we can get some of their money back over here.'"

In his State of the Union address, President Johnson pledges "war against poverty" and to carry forward John F. Kennedy's social programs.

LBJ equates the John Birch Society with the KKK.

Chamber of Commerce, Washington, D.C.

Political uncertainty in South Vietnam continues to hamper the war against the Viet Cong rebels.

THE UNITED STATES INCREASES AID TO SOUTH VIETNAM

For the first time, helicopters prove their worth as a combat weapon and are being used for observation, for strafing the enemy and for penetrating jungle areas with combat troops.

The efficiency of the Vietnamese soldiers does not extend to the government and at year's end, there is another upheaval as a group of military commanders oust the civilian government.

It is a move that meets with immediate disapproval from the United States.

The United Nations Security Council meets on the mounting crisis in Southeast Asia.

Ambassador Adlai Stevenson reaffirms the position of the United States:

"As long as the peoples of that area are determined to preserve their own independence and ask for our help in preserving it, we will extend it. This, of course, is the meaning of President Johnson's request a few days ago for additional funds for more economic as well as military assistance for Vietnam. And if anyone has the illusion, Mr. Chairman, that my government will abandon the people of Vietnam or that we should weary of the burden of support that we are rendering these people, it will be only due to ignorance of the strength and the conviction of the American people."

He continues to point out that the U.S. will withdraw from Southeast Asia once stable conditions are met:

"Stop the secret subversion of other people's independence. Stop the clandestine and illegal transit of national frontiers. Stop the export of revolution and the doctrine of violence. Stop the violations of political agreements reached at Geneva for the future of Southeast Asia. The people of Laos want to be left alone. The people of Vietnam want to be left alone. The people of Cambodia want to be left alone. When their neighbors decide to leave them alone, as they must, there will be no fighting in Southeast Asia and no need for American advisors to leave their homes to help these people with this aggression."

WHAT A YEAR IT WAS!

Getaloadathat!

Coronet 500:
The newcomer that's
a real goer.
Hot Dodge ... new lower price.
Looks outside ...
luxury inside.
Buckets on the floor,
eight under the hood.

Rarin' to go?
Grab that stick—off in a shot.
Coronet:
a far cry from the ordinary,
a whale of a car for the cost.
Drive in it ...
dream in it.
See what we mean?
Dodge comes on big for '65.

'65 Dodge Coronet

DODGE COMES ON BIG FOR '65 • DART • CORONET • POLARA • CUSTOM 880 • MONACO

DODGE DIVISION CHRYSLER MOTORS CORPORATION

9

1964 VIETNAM

LBJ rejects de Gaulle's plan for a neutral Vietnam.

U.S. to send South Vietnam an additional $50 million in aid.

Senator Barry Goldwater appears on ABC-TV proposing the use of "low-yield atomic weapons" in South Vietnam.

U.S. sends aircraft to Laos for use against Pathet Lao rebels.

600 additional U.S. troops are sent to Vietnam.

U.S. to send 5,000 more advisers to Vietnam.

The Senate and the House of Representatives vote almost unanimously to give President Johnson greater authority to strike back against the Communists in North Vietnam.

Australia starts draft to fill commitment in Vietnam.

THE HIGH COST OF WAR
(as of July 8th)

TOTAL AMERICAN CASUALTIES — 1,387

Killed in Combat	152
Noncombat Accidents	151
Noncombat Causes	96
Missing in Action	17
Wounded in Action	971

Cambodia's Prince Sihanouk blames U.S. for South Vietnamese air raid on village.

In Cambodia, protesters riot in demonstrations against U.S. and Britain.

Military dissidents led by Major General Nguyen Khanh oust Vietnam junta, replacing Major General Duong Van Minh as chairman of the Military Revolutionary Council.

Six people are wounded on General Westmoreland's plane by Viet Cong fire.

Ngo Dinh Can, brother of the late President Diem, is executed in Saigon by military junta.

All crewmen escape as Viet Cong sink USS CARD.

French Embassy in Saigon is ransacked on the 10th anniversary of the Geneva accord.

In the biggest battle yet, Viet Cong forces inflict a serious defeat on South Vietnamese government troops in the Mekong Delta region.

Guerrillas attack village four miles from Saigon.

Communist PT boats fire on U.S. destroyer in Tonkin Gulf.

U.S. planes hit bases in North Vietnam.

Two U.S. destroyers sunk in Tonkin Gulf.

North Vietnam reports downing five U.S. planes as air raids continue.

In Saigon, Nguyen Khanh agrees to share power and a triumvirate of generals is chosen to lead.

U.S. destroyers fire on hostile targets in Tonkin Gulf.

In Saigon, civilian Phan Khac Suu is installed as head of state by a military junta.

Viet Cong attack major U.S. base, destroying six B-57s.

Saigon imposes martial law to halt student riots.

South Vietnam begins biggest attack of the war striking at a Communist guerrilla stronghold in a forest 40 miles northwest of Saigon.

Three Buddhist leaders begin hunger strike in Saigon to protest the government.

Two officers die when U.S. headquarters in Saigon is hit by a bomb.

Attorney General Robert F. Kennedy and his family enjoy a riotous reception behind the Iron Curtain.

Ethel receives a bouquet from an excited admirer as people line up to catch a glimpse of one of America's favorite couples.

In Krakow, the Kennedys are mobbed by a crowd of 15,000 Poles.

Unhappy with the outpouring, the government throws a news blackout on his visit.

However, within minutes of their arrival at Jagiellonian University, word spreads throughout the city.

WHAT A YEAR IT WAS!

Observers say that Mr. Kennedy doesn't take it as a personal triumph.

The city police go on the presumption that the visit will be ignored and are ill prepared for this emotional outpouring by the Poles, who feel deep ties to the United States.

Finally, the Kennedy party takes refuge atop a Soviet-built sedan put at their disposal, where Ethel receives more flowers and signs autographs.

1964

In the Soviet Union the people have no voice in who's in and who's out.

SOVIET

KHRUSHCHEV BOUNCED FROM OFFICE

Khrushchev is yanked as Soviet Prime Minister.

Leonid Brezhnev is named new party leader.

Brezhnev receives a standing ovation from the Central Party members following his appointment.

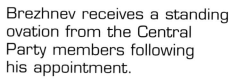

However, Nikita is still in full voice and when he visits the United Nations, his harangue leaves the delegates aghast.

WHAT A YEAR IT WAS!

UNION

WHEN WE SPEAK, MOSCOW LISTENS

American wrecking crews uncover over 40 microphones embedded in the walls of the U.S. Embassy in Moscow.

Soviets down U.S. jet over East Germany, killing three.

U.S. and U.S.S.R. sign pact to cut production of fissionable material for arms.

The International Commission of Jurists meets in Geneva and attacks Soviet repression of Jews.

Anastas Mikoyan becomes Soviet president.

Premier Khrushchev discloses that the Soviet Union is using spy satellites to photograph American military bases and installations.

In a message to Peking, new Soviet leaders call for Communist unity.

Russian students, protesting aid to the Congo, attack the U.S. Embassy in Moscow.

- **France opens ties with Communist China.**

- **Peking charges Khrushchev with seeking capitalist rule.**

- **Peking accuses Moscow of backing U.S. intervention in Vietnam.**

Chou En-lai

- **Communist China explodes its first atomic bomb, becoming the fifth nuclear power.**

- **Chou En-lai visits Moscow to mark the 47th anniversary of the Bolshevik Revolution.**

- **Communist China sends military aid to Cambodia.**

- **Eisaku Sato elected premier of Japan.**

- **Indonesia and Malaysia agree to a cease-fire.**

- **Indonesia President Sukarno tells U.S.: "To hell with your aid."**

- **74 die as U.S. military plane goes down in the Philippines.**

Sukarno

- **Martial law is declared in Seoul as 10,000 riot.**

1964

Stabbing in Tokyo

EDWIN O. REISCHAUER, U.S. Ambassador to Japan *(left)*, becomes the center of an international incident when he is stabbed at the Embassy Building in Tokyo.

The popular diplomat, who has a Japanese wife, is attacked at high noon by a young man, who scales the compound wall.

He strikes the ambassador in the chancellery hallway but is quickly subdued.

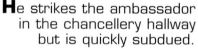

The ambassador is rushed to the hospital, suffering from a deep thigh wound and loss of blood.

Four top-flight Japanese surgeons work for 85 minutes to repair the damage and Mr. Reischauer is quickly pronounced out of danger.

There is shock in Japan over the attack, but the ambassador expresses hope that the incident will be forgotten.

The 19-year-old assailant has a long record of mental illnesses and when arrested says he is trying to focus attention on the plight of nearsighted people.

WHAT A YEAR IT WAS!

EUROPE

LBJ meets with Irish President **Eamon de Valera**.

U.N. forces land in Cyprus.

At the U.N., Turkey and Greece agree to a cease-fire.

Malta gains independence in British Commonwealth.

Willy Brandt

In West Germany, **Willy Brandt** is elected chairman of Social Democrats.

U.S. reconnaissance bomber shot down over East Germany.

Following the death of **Otto Grotewohl**, **Willi Stoph** is named premier of East Germany.

Antonin Novotny

An East German guard is killed as 57 people flee to West Germany through a tunnel.

Antonin Novotny re-elected Czech president.

CONSERVATIVES OUSTED IN GREAT BRITAIN

Sir Alec Douglas-Home *is forced to resign as Prime Minister as British voters end a 13-year Conservative Party rule.*

The Labour Party takes over at Number 10 Downing Street as **Harold Wilson** *becomes the new Prime Minister.*

1964 A TOWERING FIGURE
PASSES FROM THE WORLD SCENE

Jawaharlal Nehru became India's first prime minister when it won its independence from Great Britain and he led his country to greatness.

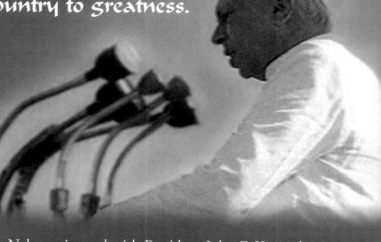

Nehru, pictured with President John F. Kennedy, was respected by world leaders and his influence was vast.

India's flag of freedom is lowered to half-mast.

Millions jam New Delhi to mourn their beloved leader.

He is accorded a Hindu funeral that calls for cremation.

Nehru has left an indelible record on the pages of history.

INDIA

In Calcutta, 200 die during Hindu-Muslim riots.

India sends troops to quell anti-Muslim violence.

500 people are seized in India as Chinese spies.

Newly elected prime minister of India Lal Bahadur Shastri names Indira Gandhi minister of information and broadcasting.

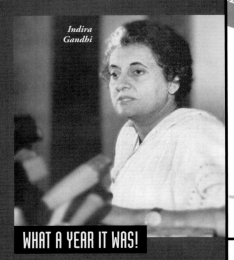

Indira Gandhi

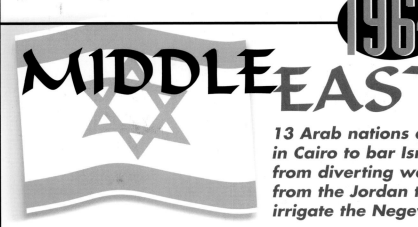

MIDDLE EAST

1964

13 Arab nations agree in Cairo to bar Israel from diverting water from the Jordan to irrigate the Negev.

Palestine National Congress meets in Jerusalem to form the PLO.

Yasser Arafat assumes leadership of Al Fatah, Arab guerrilla forces.

Iraq and Kurdish rebels enter into a cease-fire.

Syria abdicates pact of military union with Iraq.

Saudi Arabia's King Saud is stripped of power and Faisal assumes full control.

Nikita Khrushchev visits the United Arab Republic and extends new loan of $227 million.

100 people are killed on United Arab Republic ship while unloading munitions in Algeria.

Yasser Arafat

TURKEY

SYRIA

MEDITERRANEAN SEA

LEBANON
ISRAEL

IRAQ

IRAN

JORDAN

EGYPT

Nile River

SAUDI ARABIA

PERSIAN GULF

RED SEA

1964

PANAMA breaks ties with the U.S., demanding revision of canal treaty.

Anti-American demonstrations in Panama result in 29 deaths and injuries to over 70 people including six students.

President Johnson announces that the U.S. will negotiate a new canal treaty while proceeding with plans to build a modern sea-level canal across Central America or Colombia.

LBJ announces U.S. is willing to renegotiate Panama Canal treaty.

U.S. and Panama resume ties after canal dispute.

Che Guevara

Moderate **Eduardo Frei Montalva** is chosen president of Chile over People's Front candidate **Salvador Allende**.

Dozens of people are injured in Buenos Aires at a rally for exiled **Juan Perón**.

Brazil sends **Juan Perón** back to Spain, ruining his efforts to return home.

A bazooka is fired at the U.N. during **Che Guevara's** speech to the General Assembly.

HAITI

François Duvalier is decreed president of Haiti for life.
•
Mass executions are reported in Haiti.

Fidel Castro

CUBA

Three people are executed in Havana as being spies for the CIA.

The Organization of American States votes 14-5 to impose sanctions on Cuba.

Meetings between Cuban Premier Fidel Castro and Soviet leader Nikita Khrushchev tighten their ideological and commercial links, with Castro supporting the Soviet Union in its recent dispute with China.

Foreign Relations Committee Chairman J.W. Fulbright tells U.S. Senate that U.S. should relax Cold War and recognize Castro.

Castro declares that he will shoot down U.S. reconnaissance planes flying over Cuba.

Castro offers to halt aid to Latin American rebels if U.S. ceases subversive activities.

In retaliation for U.S. seizure of four Cuban fishing boats, Cuba blocks water supply to Guantanamo Bay Naval Base.

In reprisal for trading with Cuba, U.S. cuts military aid to five nations.

Castro announces he will reduce trading with non-Communist countries.

WHAT A YEAR IT WAS!

AFRICA

PRESIDENT KWAME NKRUMAH escapes fifth assassination attempt in GHANA.

Protesting anti-American actions, the U.S. recalls its ambassador to GHANA.

Following a one-day military coup, French troops restore government in GABON.

Retaliating for land seizures in TUNISIA, France suspends aid.

In its first military operation in Africa since the 1956 Suez crisis, British armed forces crush African mutinies in TANGANYIKA, KENYA and UGANDA.

KENYA becomes a republic.

U.S. agrees to give up Wheelus Air Force Base in LIBYA.

Nyasaland becomes the independent country of MALAWI within the Commonwealth.

WHAT A YEAR IT WAS!

Following the ouster of the Arab government in Zanzibar, ABEID KARUME proclaims a people's republic. The U.S. consul is seized at gunpoint.

Britain and U.S. recognize new Zanzibar government.

Tanganyika and Zanzibar unite to form the Republic of Tanzania.

IAN SMITH named prime minister by the white supremacist Rhodesian Front Party.

London appeals to Rhodesia to force resignation of Prime Minister IAN SMITH.

Ending 73 years of British rule, Northern Rhodesia becomes Republic of Zambia.

As the nation nears independence, KENNETH KAUNDA is elected president in Zambia.

Last French troops leave Algeria.

Morocco and Algeria agree to end border conflict.

Algeria receives loan from Moscow for technical assistance.

Tanzania

- International boundary
- Region boundary
- ★ National capital
- ◉ Region capital
- Railroad
- Road

150 Kilometers
150 Miles

OVER 200 HOSTAGES are freed while 20 to 30 hostages are slaughtered by rebels as Belgian paratroopers begin rescue operations in the Congo.

2,000 CONGOLESE troops open attack on rebels.

MOISE TSHOMBE, former secessionist from Katanga, is named premier of the Congo.

U.S. SENDS FOUR PLANES to Congo to aid Premier Tshombe.

Moise Tshombe

21

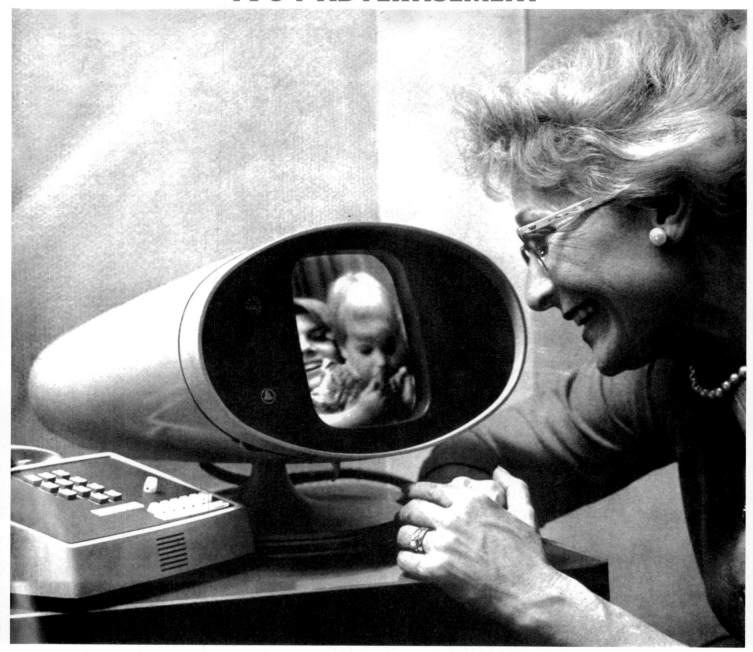

A logical extension of today's telephone service...

Bell System introduces PICTUREPHONE service

Both ends of telephone conversations are pictured; people phone by appointment from family-type booths in attended centers.

■

New York (Grand Central Station), Chicago (Prudential Building), Washington (National Geographic Society Building) have service.

Bell System PICTUREPHONE service now lets callers *see* as well as talk on the telephone. And "hands-free" if they wish.

For the first time, people can make a visual telephone call to another city—the latest example of the research, invention and development that are constantly improving the communications we provide.

The new service is being offered in the cities listed at the left. Bell System attendants at each local center help callers enjoy pre-arranged face-to-face visits with friends or relatives in either of the other cities.

Further development of PICTUREPHONE service is still in the future. But the service is another step toward our goal of providing you with better, warmer, more nearly complete communication by telephone.

Bell System *Serving you*
American Telephone & Telegraph Co. and Associated Companies

22

People

FORMER PRESIDENT
HERBERT CLARK HOOVER DIES

Herbert Clark Hoover became the 31st President of the United States in 1929, overcame the derision of being the depression president and was a consultant to his successors.

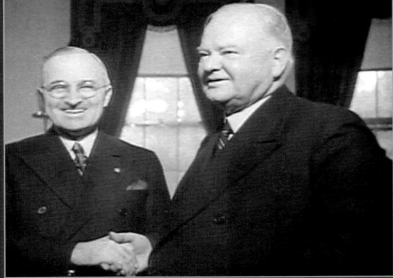

Pictured here in 1945 with President Harry S. Truman.

A grateful nation accords Mr. Hoover a state funeral, with his body resting in the rotunda of the Capitol. His was a notable record of public service.

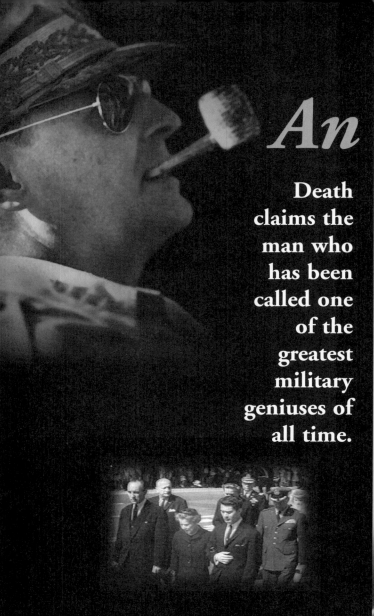

An Old Soldier

Death claims the man who has been called one of the greatest military geniuses of all time.

His wife and son lead dignitaries at a state funeral as the nation says farewell. MacArthur's passing is mourned all over the world for this was a soldier who had captured the popular imagination.

General Douglas MacArthur is greeted by a ticker-tape parade and idolized on his recall from the Korean front in 1951.

Terming him the savior of their country, Australians pay tribute to General MacArthur in 1944.

General MacArthur is greeted in 1945 by the Filipino people as he returns to inspect the damage done by Japanese forces.

Finally Fades Away

Aboard the U.S.S. *Missouri* in Tokyo Bay, on Sunday, September 2, 1945, on behalf of the United States, General MacArthur, Supreme Commander signs the Japanese surrender, bringing World War II to an official end.

Commander in chief in the Far East, he visits the fighting front in Korea in 1950.

After 14 years, in 1951 General MacArthur comes home, accompanied by his wife and son, and receives a tumultuous welcome from the crowd gathered at the San Francisco Airport to greet him.

Governor Earl Warren of California has a warm welcome for the man whose dismissal as Commander of the Far East forces stirred the nation (1951).

The U.S. Congress gives him a standing ovation (1951).

He addresses Congress, talking about his 52 years of military service, ending with his famous line: "Old soldiers never die, they just fade away" (1951).

1964

WHAT'S NEXT? A WASHING MACHINE/DRYER COMBO?

MAO TSE-TUNG joins the "foreign devils" and orders a decadent $12,726 Silver Cloud Mark III Rolls-Royce.

Iranian students demonstrate against the **SHAH OF IRAN** *(right)* as he is receiving an honorary degree from University of California at Los Angeles.

CUBA, NO — MEXICO, SI

Charging Cuban Premier **FIDEL CASTRO** with betraying Cuba to Russian imperialism and comparing his secret police with "the worst elements of the Gestapo," his sister **JUANA CASTRO RUZ** defects and seeks political asylum in Mexico.

At a dinner given for U.N. Ambassador **Adlai Stevenson** by the Eleanor Roosevelt Memorial Foundation, the 64-year-old describes the life of a diplomat as "protocol, alcohol and Geritol."

CROSSING PARTY LINES

Former presidents **Harry S. Truman** and **Dwight D. Eisenhower** are named co-chairmen of the Honorary Sponsors Council of Planned Parenthood — World Population.

Both the March of Dimes and a Miami Coast Guard Auxiliary turn down **Elvis Presley's** gift of a white yacht saying they can't afford the maintenance, but **Danny Thomas** takes the plunge and accepts it on behalf of Memphis' St. Jude's Hospital for children.

Japanese-American **Patsy Mink** is elected in Hawaii, making her the first woman from a racial or ethnic minority to sit in the House.

General William Westmoreland succeeds **General Paul Harkins** as head of U.S. forces in Vietnam.

Pope Paul VI becomes the first pontiff to ride in an airplane and travel to the Holy Land.

BRIGITTE MEETS THE PRESS

Delicious French pastry **Brigitte Bardot** *(left) is mobbed by 150 newsmen as she arrives in Rio for some rest with her Brazilian boyfriend.*

X MARKS THE SPOT

Black activist leader Malcolm X announces he is leaving the Black Muslim movement led by Elijah Muhammed to form the "black nationalist party."

Malcolm X makes a pilgrimage to Mecca.

Malcolm X forms the Organization for Afro-American Unity to seek independence for blacks in the Western Hemisphere.

Malcolm X visits Cassius Clay's training camp.

J. Edgar Hoover calls Martin Luther King Jr. the "most notorious liar in the country."

RICE (Oryza Sativa)
One of the world's most nourishing grains—a store-house of thiamine, niacin and iron

涼脆美！

In the mother tongue of rice, that says "COOLCRISPANDELICIOUS!"

Kellogg's RICE KRISPIES

"The best to you each morning"

Kennedys

Still in mourning, Jacqueline Kennedy, 34, drops by her new office in the old State Department Building to express her thanks to the 25 volunteers who have opened and organized her 700,000 letters of condolence.

Wearing black, Jackie faces television cameras in the office of Robert F. Kennedy to acknowledge all the messages of condolence received and promises they will be preserved in the $10 million John F. Kennedy Library at Harvard.

Jackie puts her 12-room Georgetown house up for sale and moves her family to New York where she can have more privacy for her and her children, John Jr. and Caroline.

10-year-old Robert F. Kennedy Jr. lists his father's occupation as "unemployed" when filling out the form for the Sidwell Friends School in Washington, D.C.

Jacqueline Kennedy leases a 10-room weekend cottage, with stables for Sardar and Macaroni, on a 47-acre enclave on Long Island's Gold Coast.

John-John Kennedy turns four and has a party with his preschool friends in his Fifth Avenue home where they feast on ice cream and cake.

Riding her horse Macaroni, six-year-old Caroline Kennedy wins sixth place at a 4-H Club show in Massachusetts.

Caroline Kennedy is enrolled at the 91st Street Academy of the Sacred Heart.

Jackie celebrates her birthday by purchasing a 15-room, $200,000 co-op on Fifth Avenue, overlooking the Central Park Reservoir.

Jackie checks into the Carlyle Hotel while her new Fifth Avenue apartment is made ready for her and Caroline and John.

A Day At The Fair

Jackie makes a surprise visit to the New York World's Fair with her daughter, Caroline, her sister-in-law Jean Kennedy Smith and Jean's children, Stephen Jr., six, and William, three.

Officially marking the end of one year of mourning, escorted by Adlai Stevenson, Jackie attends a U.N. concert commemorating the 16th anniversary of the adoption of its Declaration of Human Rights.

John F. and Jackie Kennedy

WHAT A YEAR IT WAS!

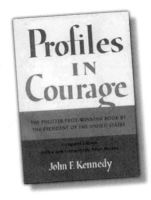

Harper & Row releases a memorial edition of John F. Kennedy's Pulitzer Prize-winning book, *Profiles in Courage.*

26 million John F. Kennedy half-dollars go on sale replacing the Benjamin Franklin coin minted in 1948.

Countries around the world issue stamps in honor of the late President John F. Kennedy.

First-day sales of the U.S. Kennedy commemorative at the Boston post office reach 2,003,096, breaking all postal cancellation records for a first day.

Following an emotional, roaring 16-minute ovation at the closing session of the 1964 Democratic National Convention, Robert F. Kennedy introduces *A Thousand Days*, a 20-minute filmed memorial to his brother's brief term in the presidency.

Robert F. Kennedy (left) and Ted Kennedy

Congress authorizes $15,500,000 toward the construction of the John F. Kennedy Center for the Performing Arts in Washington, D.C.

An estimated 8,000,000 people visit President Kennedy's grave at Arlington National Cemetery this year.

Attorney General Robert F. Kennedy announces the formation of an Office of Criminal Justice within the Justice Department whose function it is to ensure that federal law enforcement is fair and effective.

Robert F. Kennedy resigns as Attorney General to run for the U.S. Senate and is elected Senator from New York.

32-year-old junior senator from Massachusetts Teddy Kennedy takes his first steps since breaking his back in a plane crash last June.

The seven-member Warren Commission, headed by Chief Justice of the United States Earl Warren, releases its 888-page report and is unanimous in its denial that either Lee Harvey Oswald or Jack Ruby were "part of any conspiracy, domestic or foreign, to assassinate President Kennedy" and concludes that Lee Harvey Oswald acted alone.

Jack Ruby, 52, is sentenced to death for the murder of Lee Harvey Oswald.

Lee Harvey Oswald, top; Jack Ruby, right

1964

JOHNSONS' CORNER

THEY'RE MAKING ENDS MEET

A released statement of the financial assets of President Johnson and his family sets the family's net worth at $3,484,098, which includes the Texas Broadcasting Corp., ranch properties in Texas and real estate holdings.

President Lyndon Johnson, Lt. Commander during World War II when he won the Army Silver Star, resigns his commander's commission in the Naval Reserve.

LET'S BEND THE LAW ON THIS ONE

President Johnson signs a special executive order extending the mandatory retirement age to past 70 for longtime FBI director J. Edgar Hoover, allowing him to serve indefinitely.

BEATLES, NO, APPLE BLOSSOM QUEEN, YES

President Johnson doesn't allow 16-year-old Lucy to see the Beatles, but says "yes" to his youngest daughter serving as queen of the Shenandoah Apple Blossom Festival.

President Johnson picks Sargent Shriver to head anti-poverty drive.

Lady Bird Johnson launches a series of White House luncheons for "women doers" and Helen Hayes, along with 13 mostly political wives, attends the opening luncheon.

THIS BIRD FLEW THE COOP

Well it's official. The engagement of 20-year-old Lynda Bird Johnson to Navy Lt. Bernard Rosenbach is kaput and that's that.

In her address to 2,000 female students at Texas Woman's University, Lady Bird Johnson tells them: "It is a good time to be a woman. It is a good time to be alive."

Winston Churchill

British Prime Minister **Sir Alec Douglas-Home**, former Prime Minister **Harold Macmillan** and Labour Party leader **Harold Wilson** are among the many leaders paying tribute to the feeble, but still highly spirited, 89-year-old **Sir Winston Churchill**, who, after 64 years in Parliament, is retiring. Not since the Duke of Wellington retired more than a century ago has a national figure been so honored—a man who became a legend in his lifetime.

Sir Winston Churchill turns 90 and his birthday cake is inscribed with the words on the flyleaf of his history of World War II:

*In war—resolution; in defeat—defiance;
in victory—magnanimity; in peace—good will.*

Former President **Harry S. Truman** turns 80, the sixth U.S. president to reach that age, and is flooded with good wishes, including a call from President **Lyndon Johnson** who jokes about wanting to call collect but said **Lady Bird** wouldn't let him.

Harry S. Truman

With his family around him, **Herbert Hoover** celebrates his 90th birthday, becoming the first U.S. president to live to this age since John Adams.

A bit cranky and in ill health, **Somerset Maugham** turns 90.

THE LITTLE TRAMP STILL WANTS US TO LAUGH

Charlie Chaplin turns 70 and wonders why the world is so serious these days and insists that he is still full of fun.

Somerset Maugham

REMOVE SOME OF THOSE CANDLES, FELLAS

Cutting her birthday cake, the last of the red-hot mamas, **Sophie Tucker**, denies turning 80, declaring she's only 76.

WHAT A YEAR IT WAS!

Princess Margaret

Royal goings-on

Princess Margaret gives birth to her second child, **Lady Sarah Armstrong-Jones**, who is seventh in the line of succession to the British throne.

63-year-old **Queen Mother Elizabeth** of England is recuperating following an appendectomy.

The **Duke of Windsor** celebrates his 70th birthday by attending an 18th-century costume ball given in his honor by **Countess Sheila de Rochambeau** at her chateau outside Paris.

Two Royal Thumbs-Up

In a speech delivered to the Foreign Press Association, Britain's **Prince Philip** approves "Beatlemania" saying that he didn't care how much noise people make singing and dancing and only objects to the noise of people fighting and stealing. He adds: "It seems to me that these blokes are helping people to enjoy themselves, and that is far better than the other thing."

The **Duke of Edinburgh** greets **the Beatles** at a fancy event at London's Empire Ballroom and offers to swap his book *(Seabirds in Southern Waters)* with author **John Lennon** *(In His Own Write)*.

Don't Get Jumpy Now

Representing her school for the first time at a local meet, 13-year-old **Princess Anne** takes her horse over the jumps winning a red rose as part of the winning team.

Britain's 15-year-old Crown Prince joins his dad, **The Prince of Wales**, in his first polo match.

Prince Charles is at a nursing home with a mild case of pneumonia.

Let's Hope There's No Sibling Rivalry

Queen Elizabeth and **Prince Philip** name their six-week-old son **Prince Edward Antony Richard Louis**, who is third in line of succession to the British throne.

PRINCE RAINIER and "with child" PRINCESS GRACE, DAVID NIVEN and the BEGUM AGA KHAN are among the celebrities attending the Red Cross charity ball in Monte Carlo.

Princess Grace

46-year-old QUEEN FREDERIKA of Greece arrives in New York with PRINCESS IRENE, 21, for a 17-day visit to the U.S.

KING PAUL I of Greece dies and is succeeded by his 23-year-old son CONSTANTINE II, who assumes the throne amid growing anti-monarchism.

Greece's dashing bachelor KING CONSTANTINE crashes his Thunderbird into the back of a fire engine, but he and his 22-year-old sister PRINCESS IRENE emerge unscathed.

Luxembourg's GRAND DUCHESS CHARLOTTE voluntarily abdicates the throne in favor of her son, CROWN PRINCE JEAN, ending her 45-year reign.

The Imperial Household chooses 24-year-old HANAKO TSUGARU to marry Japan's 28-year-old PRINCE YOSHI, the Emperor's younger son, and the couple is wed in a traditional Shinto ceremony.

Queen Elizabeth

1964 POLICE BLOTTER

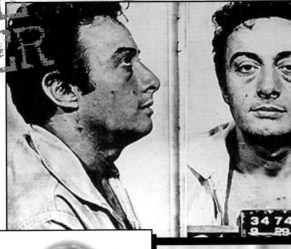

THE BOOKIE DIDN'T GET BOOKED

The New York Civil Liberties Union calls the arrest of rich old racketeer **Frank Costello** on vagrancy charges, while lunching with friends at a Broadway eatery, "an outrage." The judge agrees and dismisses the complaint.

NOW YOU SEE HIM, NOW YOU DON'T

Joseph Bonanno or "Joe Bananas," alleged leader of a Brooklyn "Cosa Nostra" gang, is kidnapped as he leaves his attorney's Park Avenue apartment house.

THIS LADY'S NOT FOR ROBBING

92-year-old cosmetic queen **Helena Rubinstein** screams her head off and refuses to cooperate with burglars who break into her New York apartment demanding access to her safe. They finally give up, tie her up with a bedsheet and take a powder (hopefully a good shade).

New York Representative **Adam Clayton Powell Jr.**, whose arrest was postponed until the House went into recess, is arrested for being "flagrantly contemptuous" of the court stemming from his failure to appear at a hearing on a $46,500 judgment brought against him in a defamation of character suit.

Top: Lenny Bruce
Above: Frank Costello
Right: Jimmy Hoffa

Despite the claims of defense attorneys that the kidnapping of **Frank Sinatra Jr.** was a publicity stunt, two men are sentenced to life for the crime.

DO THE WORDS "FREEDOM OF SPEECH" MEAN ANYTHING?

Ailing **Lenny Bruce** goes on trial in New York City on obscenity charges for using foul language.

100 people protest the arrest of Lenny Bruce.

Mario Savio, leader of the Free Speech Movement at the University of California at Berkeley, is arrested by campus police as thousands of students and professors watch in shock as he's dragged away from the microphone.

RIDDLE ME THIS

Despite being convicted twice of serious crimes and remaining free on bail while his attorneys pursue appeals, the International Brotherhood of Teamsters President **James R. Hoffa** holds onto his job.

James R. Hoffa is fined $10,000 and sentenced to eight years in prison following his conviction on charges of jury-tampering.

James Hoffa denounces as a lie a report that he had threatened to kill Attorney General **Robert F. Kennedy**.

- - - - - - - - -

Teamster **Dave Beck** completes 30 months of his five-year term for cheating on his tax returns.

WHAT A YEAR IT WAS!

New! Pre-sweetened Kool-Aid

"Isn't it great—now we don't have to add any sugar!"

It's sweetened **without** sugar to give you all the benefits and convenience of artificial sweetening. You just add water and ice —so it costs no more to make than regular Kool-Aid.
Now two kinds of Kool-Aid—new pre-sweetened *and* regular. Both make two quarts of pure, wholesome refreshment.

Awards & Rewards

THE CONQUERING HERO RETURNS

Japan bestows the Order of the Grand Cordon of the Rising Sun on **GENERAL CURTIS LEMAY**, U.S. Air Force Chief of Staff and World War II Bomber Command head, for his role in building up the country's postwar defenses.

• NBC-TV newscaster **DAVID BRINKLEY** gets the 1964 Golden Key Award by the American Association of School Administrators.

• Commemorating the 22nd anniversary of the Battle of Bataan, Long Island University drapes the aqua-colored hood of a doctor of letters on **GENERAL DOUGLAS MACARTHUR**, making this his 17th honorary degree.

David Brinkley

• Elks Lodge No. 27 of Memphis, Tennessee awards **ELVIS PRESLEY** their Americanism award "for setting a flawless example for American youth in all that he does and says."

• Army **CAPTAIN ROGER H.C. DONLON**, wounded four times in South Vietnam, receives the Congressional Medal of Honor for "conspicuous gallantry" during battle.

• Returning to New York, Nobel prize winner **REV. MARTIN LUTHER KING JR.** receives a hero's welcome from Mayor Robert Wagner who presents him with a Medallion of Honor and says: "This city has welcomed many world-renowned figures, but I can think of none who has won a more lasting place in the moral epic of America."

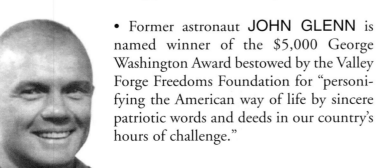

• Former astronaut **JOHN GLENN** is named winner of the $5,000 George Washington Award bestowed by the Valley Forge Freedoms Foundation for "personifying the American way of life by sincere patriotic words and deeds in our country's hours of challenge."

John Glenn

WHERE THERE'S HOPE

61-year-old comedian **Bob Hope** receives the **National Citizenship Award of the Military Chaplains Association** for his "tireless, unselfish efforts" to bring "warmth and cheer by personal visits" to U.S. servicemen.

Bob Hope and his entertainment troupe arrive in South Vietnam just as the U.S. officers' quarters are bombed on December 24th and he immediately visits the wounded.

Replacing **Henry Cabot Lodge**, **Bob Hope** is appointed to the 10-member board that selects winners of the **Presidential Medal of Freedom**.

PLAYGROUND OF IGUANAS & THE RICH & FAMOUS

Honorary mayor of Palm Springs **Bob Hope** jokes that "nobody dies in Palm Springs."

Dolores Hope is chosen as the **Chicago Notre Dame Club's Woman of the Year**.

WHAT A YEAR IT WAS!

Presidential
Medal of Freedom
(Nation's Highest Civilian Honor)
──────── a sampling ────────

Dean Acheson	*Former Secretary of State*
Carl Vinson	*U.S. Representative (Georgia)*
Edward R. Murrow	*Former TV Commentator*
Aaron Copland	*Composer*
Walt Disney	*Animation Pioneer*
James Frank Dobie	*Author*
Lena F. Edwards	*Physician & Humanitarian*
T.S. Eliot	*Author & Nobel Laureate*
Willem de Kooning	*Artist*
John L. Lewis	*President, United Mine Workers of America*
Walter Lippmann	*Journalist & Author*
Alfred Lunt & Lynn Fontanne	*Theater's Husband & Wife Team*
Leontyne Price	*Concert & Opera Singer*
Carl Sandburg	*Poet & Biographer*
John Steinbeck	*Author, Playwright & Nobel Laureate*
Thomas J. Watson Jr.	*President, IBM*
Helen Keller	*Deaf, Mute & Blind Leading Figure in Effort to Assist the Blind*

Edward R. Murrow

Lady Bird Johnson

Walt Disney

LBJ

MAN
OF THE
YEAR
(Gallup Poll)

President Lyndon B. Johnson

Winston Churchill

Dwight D. Eisenhower
(former president)

Martin Luther King Jr.

MOST ADMIRED
WOMAN
OF THE
YEAR

Jacqueline Kennedy
(third consecutive year)

Lady Bird Johnson
(First Lady)

TIME
MAN
OF THE
YEAR

President Lyndon B. Johnson

Architect
OF THE
YEAR

Edward Durell Stone (62)

Ills of the RICH & FAMOUS

89-year-old former **President Herbert Hoover** is recovering following a respiratory infection and bleeding right kidney.

John Glenn is in the hospital with a mild concussion that he sustained from a fall in his bathroom while trying to fix a loose cabinet. He subsequently withdraws his candidacy for U.S. Senator due to his injury.

Spencer Tracy is ill with a continuing respiratory ailment complicated by diabetes.

75-year-old New York World's Fair President **Robert Moses** is recovering from prostate surgery.

Dwight Eisenhower is at Washington's Walter Reed Hospital with an inflammation of the respiratory tract.

Harry S. Truman, 80, fractures two ribs and cuts his forehead after falling in his bathtub.

18-year-old **Hayley Mills** leaves her sickbed with a high temperature to perform in the chorus line at a London benefit where she demonstrates some unDisney-like bumps and grinds.

X-rated "bad boy" comedian **Lenny Bruce** is in fair condition following surgery in New York for pleurisy in his left lung.

Spencer Tracy

TAYLOR, FISHER & BURTON (NOT A LAW FIRM)

Dick, Liz and Eddie

A BLOODY INTERVENTION
Richard Burton, with a little coaxing from his wife, **Elizabeth Taylor**, establishes the Richard Burton Hemophilia Fund to help battle the blood disease.

HELL NO, SHE WON'T PAY
Insults are being hurled back and forth between **Elizabeth Taylor**, **Richard Burton** and **Eddie Fisher**, who is demanding a $1 million divorce settlement from his estranged wife.

Just 10 days after getting a divorce from **Eddie Fisher**, 32-year-old **Elizabeth Taylor** marries **Richard Burton** in Montreal.

HEIRESS TO BAREFOOT PRINCESS
51-year-old Woolworth heiress **Barbara Hutton** marries 48-year-old Laotian painter-chemist **Prince Raymond Doan Vinh Na Champassak** in a shoeless ceremony at her Mexican estate, making him her seventh husband.

HAPPY ISN'T HAPPY
Mrs. Nelson Rockefeller loses her custody battle, and her ex-husband is awarded custody of their children.

WHAT A YEAR IT WAS!

Passings

KING PAUL OF GREECE, 62
Beloved ruler of Greece.

LADY NANCY ASTOR, 84
American-born socialite, first woman in Britain's House of Commons, famous for her witty sayings, including one about marriage: "I married beneath me. All women do."

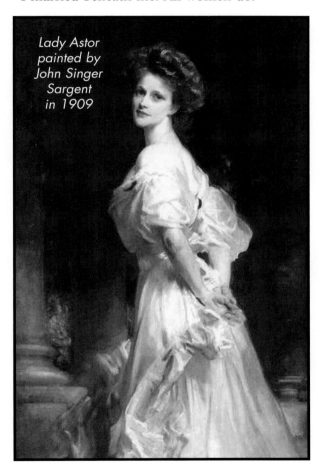

Lady Astor painted by John Singer Sargent in 1909

HARRY GROSSINGER, 76
Founder and proprietor of the famed Catskill resort Grossinger's, a favorite of entertainers.

SGT. ALVIN CULLUM YORK, 76
World War I hero who on one day in 1918 killed 25 and captured 132 German soldiers. He later received dozens of medals including the Congressional Medal of Honor.

1964 Coupling

Alan Arkin & Barbara Dana

Charlie Watts & Shirley Ann Arnold

Janet Gaynor & Paul Gregory

Anna Maria Alberghetti & Claudio Guzman

Chubby Checker & Catherina Lodders

Margaret Leighton & Michael Wilding

Beau Bridges & Julie Landifield

Edie Adams & Marty Mills

Jayne Mansfield & Matt Cimber

Bill Cosby & Camille Hanks

Elizabeth Taylor & Richard Burton

Joan Didion & John Gregory Dunne

Mel Brooks & Anne Bancroft

Billy Rose & Doris Warner Vidor

Elke Sommer & Joe Hyams

Miriam Makeba & Hugh Masekela

Bob Newhart & Virginia Quinn

Ethel Merman & Ernest Borgnine

Joan Fontaine & Alfred Wright Jr.

Brian Wilson & Marilyn Rovell

Gloria Vanderbilt & Wyatt Cooper

Michael Nesmith & Phyllis Barbour

Judy Garland & Mark Herron

Bruce Lee & Linda Emery

Harrison Ford & Mary Marquardt

John Coltrane & Alice Macleod

Lew Ayres & Diana Hall

Muhammad Ali **&** Sonji Roi

Peggy Lee **&** Jack Del Rio

Peter Benchley **&** Winifred Wesson

Peter Sellers **&** Britt Ekland

Red Buttons **&** Alicia Pratt

Roy Campanella **&** Roxie Doles

Tippi Hedren **&** Noel Marshall

Troy Donahue **&** Suzanne Pleshette

Royal Weddings

King Constantine of the Hellenes **&** Princess Anne-Marie of Denmark

Princess Desiree of Sweden **&** Baron Niclas Silfverschiold

Prince Yoshi of Japan **&** Hanako Tsugaru

Princess Margaretha of Sweden **&** John K. Ambler

Princess Irene of the Netherlands **&** Prince Carlos Hugo of Bourbon-Parma

Uncoupling

Arlene Dahl **&** Chris Holmes

George Peppard **&** Helen Davies

Troy Donahue **&** Suzanne Pleshette

Dinah Shore **&** Maurice Smith

James Mason **&** Pamela Mason

Dorothy Malone **&** Jacques Bergerac

Les Paul **&** Mary Ford

Xavier Cugat **&** Abbe Lane

Elizabeth Taylor **&** Eddie Fisher

Marjorie Merriweather Post Close Hutton Davies **&** Herbert May

Ethel Merman **&** Ernest Borgnine

Sammy Cahn **&** Gloria Delson Cahn

NEW
GAINES·BURGERS

the canned dog food...
without the can

Gaines·burgers is a registered trade-mark of General Foods Corp.

Two Gaines·burgers are equal in nourishment to a one-pound can of the finest canned dog foods, and they cost no more. They may look like less, but that's because they do not have all the water found in canned dog foods.

So convenient! These soft, beefy burgers come in an easy-to-carry, easy-to-store box, have no odor—and need no refrigeration! Keep them in the kitchen cabinet, even after you've opened the box.

Gaines·burgers unique new formula gives your dog everything he is known to need and like. He gets beef, a vegetable, minerals, milk solids and vitamins in appetizing burger form. New Gaines·burgers are a fully satisfying, fully balanced daily diet.

Feeding is easy. Just break Gaines·burgers into a dish, set before your dog. Nothing to scoop, scrape, mash, or spill. If you've been feeding 1 can a day, give him 2 Gaines·burgers; if 2 cans, 4 Gaines·burgers, and so on. To complete his meal, serve water alongside. New Gaines·burgers are a whole new way to feed your dog every day. And you can buy them six to the package (nourishment equal to 3 one-pound cans) or the more convenient way: 12 to the package.

GENERAL FOODS

40

Human Interest

WORLD'S MOST POPULAR GOOD-LUCK CHARM

"Dammit" doll *(replacing the rabbit's foot)*

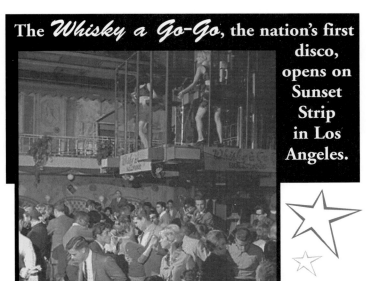

The *Whisky a Go-Go*, the nation's first disco, opens on Sunset Strip in Los Angeles.

Every Which Way And Up

With their new ability to change direction, skateboards reach a new popularity.

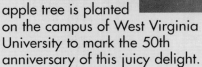

GETTING HIS ROCKS OFF

New York jeweler **Harry Winston** donates a 253.7-carat uncut stone to the Smithsonian, the second such gift, the first one being the 44.5-carat Hope Diamond he donated in 1958.

Chinese New Year marks the year 4662— *Year of the Dragon.*

DIG YOUR TEETH INTO THIS ONE

A *Golden Delicious* apple tree is planted on the campus of West Virginia University to mark the 50th anniversary of this juicy delight.

LEANING A BIT TOO FAR?

An Italian scientist says the *Tower of Pisa* may fall at any time.

CAN 90210 BE FAR BEHIND?

To increase efficiency in sorting, a few large eastern post offices begin using *ZIP codes.*

Mr. ZIP

WHAT A YEAR IT WAS!

41

1964

NEW YORK

1964 1965 WORLD'S FAIR

UNISPHERE®

Soaring 12 stories above the New York World's Fair, the stainless steel Unisphere makes its official debut as the symbol of the most ambitious exposition ever attempted. Set in 646 acres, this billion-dollar structure opens its doors to an expected 70 million people.

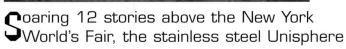

Although 29 million tickets have been sold, rain on opening day cuts the number of visitors to only 92,000 against an expected quarter million.

INTERNATIONAL PLAZA

It wouldn't be a World's Fair without offering a world tour right here in New York. Want to visit Hong Kong?

The International Plaza offers a sampling of life in countries many of us never even hope to visit.

You can go east to Pakistan *[left]* and when you've seen every-thing there, detour to Japan *[below]*.

Visitors can take a side trip to Thailand *[left]*, then India *[below]* and finally a visit to the Philippines *[right]*.

WHAT A YEAR IT WAS!

From Berlin back across the sea to Hollywood and all the glamour of the movie capital.

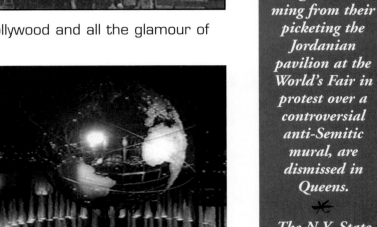

When night falls, the grounds are transformed into a fairy-land with the Unisphere bathed in shimmering lights and encircled by dancing waters.

Disorderly conduct charges against 12 leaders of the American Jewish Congress, stemming from their picketing the Jordanian pavilion at the World's Fair in protest over a controversial anti-Semitic mural, are dismissed in Queens.

✳

The N.Y. State Supreme Court rules that no matter how "regrettable" the Jordanian mural might be, there is no legal basis to compel Jordan or New York City to remove it.

✳

Police arrest at least 300 civil rights activists during the opening day of the New York World's Fair. New York Governor Nelson A. Rockefeller criticizes the demonstrations.

THE NUMBERS

The Canadian House of Commons votes to replace the Canadian red ensign flag, with a British Union Jack in one corner, with one with a new Canadian design, a large red maple leaf in a white center with a red vertical stripe at each end.

A new round of negotiations, known as "Kennedy Round," aimed at cutting world tariffs, opens in Geneva.

ENOUGH BORSCHT & BEATINGS
KGB aide Yuri I. Nossenko defects from the Soviet Union and seeks political asylum in the U.S.

Easter violence between Mods and Rockers disturbs British sea resorts.

HEY MAN, NOW I HAVE TO KICK THE POTATO CHIP HABIT

Kenya becomes the 40th state to ratify the U.N.'s 1961 Convention of Narcotics Drugs banning the eating or smoking of opium, the chewing of the coca leaf and the use of marijuana or hashish.

An electronic voting system has been installed in the U.N. General Assembly replacing voice vote country by country.

Facing severe internal stresses that could jeopardize its very existence, NATO marks its 15th anniversary.

THAT'S A LOT OF HAMBURGERS & FRIES
American teenagers number 22 million and are growing as a group three times faster than the total population.

With the U.S. population growth dropping to its slowest pace for any year since 1946-1947, the Census Bureau estimates the population at around 190,695,000.

An estimated 220 babies are being born every minute.

PUT THAT TOILET SEAT DOWN, BOYS
Mrs. Walter Earl, of Bryan, Texas, gives birth to the first girl born into the Earl family in 300 years.

SATURDAY NIGHT COULD BE THE LONELIEST NIGHT OF THE WEEK
Projections indicate that by 1975, women will outnumber men 136 to 100, or around 2,000,000 more women than men.

WHERE THE PEOPLE ARE
Top 10 Most Populated Cities

Tokyo	(Japan)
New York	(U.S.)
Shanghai	(China)
Moscow	(U.S.S.R.)
Bombay	(India)
São Paulo	(Brazil)
Peking	(China)
Cairo	(United Arab Republic)
Leningrad	(U.S.S.R.)
Rio de Janeiro	(Brazil)

WORLDWIDE PER CAPITA INCOME
(Based on the United Nations survey of 143 countries)

Less than $500 in 115 countries

Waxing Poetic — 1964

Nikita Khrushchev approaches Canadian customs en route to Niagara Falls.

The top Red has nothing to declare and is waved through.

Khrushchev is here to attend the opening of a branch of Madame Tussaud's famous wax museum, with a full roster of startlingly lifelike effigies of the famous and infamous.

There's a bit of spectator confusion at the falls *(below)* at the image of Father Hennepin, who was the first European to sketch and record the national waters.

So lifelike it's hard to believe he's only wax!

LBJ pledges that *"we will not permit any part of America to become a jungle, where the weak are the prey of the strong and the many."*

CIVIL RIGHTS
THE GOOD, THE BAD & THE UGLY

IT'S *MISS* HAMILTON TO YOU!

Mary Hamilton, a black field secretary for the Congress of Racial Equality, wins her contempt case when the Supreme Court rules that addressing blacks by their first names, without the prefix of Mr., Mrs. or Miss, is a form of racial discrimination.

• The 24th Amendment to the U.S. Constitution is ratified abolishing the poll tax, which the south has used to disenfranchise poor blacks since the Civil War.

• The U.S. Supreme Court invalidates a Louisiana law requiring that a candidate's race be listed on the ballot.

• In a historic decision, the U.S. Supreme Court rules that congressional districts must be substantially equal in population, translating into "one person, one vote."

• The U.S. Supreme Court rules that a Florida law banning racially mixed couples from living together is an unconstitutional violation of the 14th Amendment's equal protection clause.

• The Justice Department files suits in Selma and Dallas County, Alabama, charging that officials have violated the 1964 Civil Rights Act "by preventing desegregation of public accommodations and of interfering with the exercise by Negroes of their right to vote."

NOBEL PEACE PRIZE
Martin Luther King Jr.

J. Raymond Jones, 65, is the new leader of Tammany Hall, the New York County Democratic organization, making him the first black to be named a county leader in the city or the state.

Capt. Lloyd Sealy becomes the first black to command a police precinct in Harlem.

Mrs. Charlotte Moton Hubbard is sworn in at the State Department as deputy assistant secretary of state for public affairs, the highest federal post ever held by a black woman.

Chaney, Schwerner and Goodman

Following their arrest for speeding and subsequent release, three civil rights activists missing in Mississippi—**James E. Chaney**, 21, **Michael Schwerner**, 24, and **Andrew Goodman**, 21—are found dead, hidden in an earthen dam.

Two residents of Philadelphia, Mississippi are indicted and arrested for the slayings of the three civil rights workers discovered two months ago.

Twenty-one men, including a sheriff and deputy, all members of the Ku Klux Klan segregationist lynch mobs, have been arrested by federal agents in connection with the brutal slayings of the three civil rights workers near Jackson, Mississippi.

Making their first arrests under the Civil Rights Act, FBI agents arrest three Mississippi whites for beating a black man who was attempting to integrate a theater in Greenwood.

Four law enforcement officials are arrested in Mississippi on charges of depriving seven blacks of their civil rights by unlawfully detaining and physically abusing them.

ENGLAND YES, FLORIDA NO
With 10% of the nation's hotels refusing to book people of Jewish descent, including 80 hotels in Arizona and Florida alone, more and more Jewish-Americans are vacationing abroad.

NEXT STOP: FLORIDA?
2,000 U.S. Protestant and Roman Catholic clergymen protest in Beverly Hills, California against Soviet persecution of Jews.

Over 1,000 students from 13 colleges and universities in the New York area picket the Soviet mission to the U.N. on May Day protesting anti-Semitism in the Soviet Union.

14 major Atlanta hotels and motels agree to accept reservations regardless of race.

Washington & Lee University in Lexington, Virginia announces that the university's board of trustees has decided to abandon its policy of barring blacks.

17 black first graders are integrated for the first time into a Biloxi, Mississippi school.

ENCOUNTERING THE WHITE COUNTER

Rev. Martin Luther King Jr. and 17 others are arrested for trying to integrate a Florida restaurant.

Protesting de facto segregation, two massive one-day civil rights school boycotts are held in New York, with one million mostly black and Puerto Rican students staying home. This was followed by a two-day boycott, by primarily white parents groups, against specific integration measures.

86% of black students participate in a school boycott in Cleveland.

Thousands riot in Harlem and in the Bedford-Stuyvesant section of Brooklyn, breaking windows and looting stores, following the killing of **James Powell**, a 15-year-old black boy, by **Lt. Thomas R. Gilligan**, an off-duty police officer. Over 100 people are injured, including 35 policemen, and 200 are arrested. **President Johnson** orders a full inquiry. Gilligan is subsequently absolved of wrongdoing in the fatal shooting.

Governor Nelson Rockefeller sends in 1,000 National Guardsmen as racial violence rips through Rochester, New York, marking the first serious race riots in the north.

Three days of race riots end in the towns of Patterson and Elizabeth, New Jersey.

In the first legal test of the 1964 Civil Rights Act, Atlanta restaurant owner **Lester Maddox** is ordered to admit blacks.

STICKS & STONES WON'T BREAK HIS BONES

Senator Barry Goldwater, Republican presidential candidate, is facing the most vitriolic attacks both domestically and worldwide, being called such names as "caveman," "hothead," "warmonger," "Neanderthal" and "ignorant bully."

THIS GOLD IS DEFINITELY ANYTHING BUT GLITTERING

Visiting in West Berlin, the Rev. Dr. Martin Luther King Jr. declares that if Senator Goldwater is elected president, "violence and riots, the like of which we have never seen before" would erupt. He also deplores "dangerous signs of Hitlerism" in Goldwater's program.

THEY'D RATHER SWITCH THAN USE NUKES

The *New York Herald Tribune* endorses a Democrat (Lyndon B. Johnson) for the first time in 123 years as do the staunch Republican *Kansas City Star* and the Hearst and Scripps-Howard newspaper chains.

John Birch Society founder Robert H.W. Welch Jr. claims that Americans who voted for President Johnson voted for "scrapping the United States Constitution" and that "the civil rights campaign was the most important and integral part of the long-range Communist plan for gradual take-over of the United States."

R. Sargent Shriver Jr., Peace Corps chief, recruits over 10,000 corpsmen serving in 46 countries, which include at least 2,000 blue-collar craftsmen as well as teachers and agricultural experts.

FATHER OF THE YEAR

R. Sargent Shriver Jr.

R. Sargent Shriver Jr.

Director of the Office of Economic Opportunity R. Sargent Shriver Jr. announces the formation of a new credit service for low-income rural families that will offer loans of up to $2,500 for financing small family businesses, trades, services and farming projects.

In New York, Dr. George James calls poverty the number three cause of deaths in the U.S.

U.S. Senate approves $1.6 billion in aid for Appalachia.

PRESIDENT JOHNSON DECLARES WAR ON POVERTY

The $1 billion Economic Opportunity Act (the anti-poverty bill) becomes law and is considered a milestone in child welfare. A major component is the Job Corps, which calls for enrolling 40,000 men and women between the ages of 16–21 who have not completed high school who would then be taught basic skills in reading, arithmetic, science, technology and citizenship.

STAMPING OUT HUNGER

President Johnson signs the Food Stamp Act to expand the pilot food stamp program established by President Kennedy in 1961 into a permanent federal and state program.

WHAT A YEAR IT WAS!

MISS WORLD
Ann Sidney (20) (Former Miss United Kingdom)

MOTHER OF THE YEAR
Mrs. Cora Hjertaas Stavig Sioux Falls, South Dakota

ON HIS HONOR HE WILL TRY
IBM chairman 50-year-old Thomas J. Watson Jr. is named president of the National Council of Boy Scouts of America.

Mrs. Mary Ingraham Bunting, president of Radcliffe College, becomes the first woman to be appointed a member of the U.S. Atomic Energy Commission.

Congress passes the $375 million Urban Mass Transportation Act of 1964 to help public and private transit companies provide and improve urban mass transportation.

The U.S. Post Office deletes the time from postmarks to cut processing time, but retains the a.m./p.m. designation.

The U.S. Supreme Court rules that the U.S. cannot legally question foreign expropriation of property.

WHO'S WATCHING THE BILL OF RIGHTS?
Despite opposition from civil rights groups and the American Bar Association, New York Governor Nelson A. Rockefeller signs into law a "stop-and-frisk" bill permitting policemen to detain a person in a public place if he "reasonably" suspects him of having committed a felony or serious misdemeanor and a "no-knock" bill allowing a policeman to obtain a search warrant from the courts for use without advance notice to occupants of a building.

1964

PLEASE STORE ALL YOUR CARRY-ON WEAPONS IN THE OVERHEAD BINS
President Johnson approves a project for the development of the largest plane in the world, a military cargo plane, to be designated CX, capable of carrying 500-700 people or 600 armed infantrymen.

The G.I. Bill of Rights celebrates its 20th anniversary.

FOUR SCORE AND MANY BLIZZARDS AGO
Marking the Civil War Centennial, a symposium on Lincoln's Gettysburg Address is held in Washington, D.C. despite one of the worst blizzards in years.

LBJ orders study to determine need for the draft.

Into The Digits He Goes
President Johnson's phone number has been changed from National 8-1414 to 456-1414.

CHEAPER BY THE DOZEN  PLUS FOUR

On the door, the traditional symbol of a new arrival in the house and on the step, six bottles of milk.

Ruby has just made a whopping big delivery of 16 puppies and she's a bit overwhelmed.

But here's a helping hand just when Ruby needs it.

Feeding 16 puppies is just too much for this tired momma, so her owners take over the feeding, which means milk by the gallon.

U.S. PET POPULATION

Dogs & Cats	54 Million
Parakeets & Canaries	1 Million
Assorted Snakes, Monkeys, Hamsters, Etc.	1 Million
Aquariums	23 Million
Tropical Fish in the Aquariums	650 Million
Amount Spent in Care & Feeding of These Pets:	$3 Billion

LAST JUMP FOR CHECKERS
Richard Nixon's black-and-white cocker spaniel, Checkers, referred to in Nixon's famous "Checkers speech" in 1952, dies at age 12.

SOMETHING TO BARK ABOUT
American Kennel Club figures show the poodle retaining its position as the most popular breed of dog in the U.S., followed by German shepherds, beagles, dachshunds and chihuahuas.

THREE SQUARES A DAY AND A ROOF WHEN IT RAINS
Animals at the Bronx Zoo, America's largest zoo, live longer and healthier lives than their counterparts living in the wild.

Mrs. John F. Kennedy presents a pair of fallow deer to New York's Central Park Zoo.

WHAT A YEAR IT WAS!

Greetings From Sunny Southern California

1964

GO WEST, YOUNG MEN – AND THEY DID
California officially becomes No. 1 in population, edging out New York, which has held that position since 1810.

Los Angeles accounted for almost one-fourth of the nation's new housing starts this year.

COUGH, COUGH, SPUTTER, SPUTTER
California's anti-smog authorities approve four $50 to $120 exhaust-control devices for mandatory installation on all 1966 model cars sold in the state.

The Pavillion, the first of a three-building cultural hub, opens in downtown Los Angeles.

YOU DON'T HAVE TO WALK A MILE FOR A DIP OR A DOLLAR
Palm Springs, California boasts more millionaires per square mile and more swimming pools per capita (around 3,100, or one for every five residents) than any other U.S. community.

Beverly Hills, California
Celebrating Its 50th Anniversary

BEVERLY HILLS™

THE STATS

No. of Psychiatrists:	198 (one for every 166 residents)
Nicknames:	"Couch Canyon" and "Libido Lane"
No. of Telephones:	50,000 for 14,300 residents (highest number of any community in the world)
Average Income:	$19,000+
Median Age:	46.8 (the oldest of any major California city)
Heavy Industry:	None
Banks:	22
Hotels:	9
Jail:	1 (cleanest in the country)
Slums:	None
Pool Hall:	None
Fencing Academy:	1
Nightlife:	None
Laundromat:	None

BETTER THAN "NEW AMSTERDAM, NEW AMSTERDAM, A WONDERFUL TOWN"
New York is celebrating its tercentenary commemorating the 1664 renaming of New Amsterdam to New York for the Duke of York.

Carnegie Hall is designated a National Historic Landmark by the Department of the Interior, thus protecting it from demolition.

— CRUISING DOWN THE RIVER ON A SUNNY AFTERNOON —
Thousands of people fill the Iowa, Illinois and Wisconsin shores to witness the first commercial riverboat race on the upper Mississippi in this century.

Foreign visitors to the U.S. reach a record high.

WHAT A YEAR IT WAS!

The air conditioner for bedrooms. The "Thinette" by General Electric.
Now $119.95*

Install "Thinette" yourself. It operates on 115 volts. Just plug it into any adequately wired circuit and be cool tonight. Easy to handle,

weighs only 67 lbs. Fits any standard sash window. Easy to remove for winter storage. Very quiet, very effective about cooling and dehumidi-

fying. Filters out dust and pollen. Now $119.95. Made for bedrooms. One of a complete line of air conditioners at your G.E. dealer's.

*Model RP 204A—4,000 B.T.U.'s. Minimum Fair Trade Price where applicable.
General Electric Company, Air Conditioning Dept., Louisville, Ky.

GENERAL ⊛ ELECTRIC

Crimes and Misdemeanors

1964

WHAT? NO MORE HANGINGS IN THE TOWN SQUARE?

England's House of Commons votes to ban the death penalty.

THE HANGING JUDGE PACKS HIS BAGS

Oregon voters abolish the death penalty, making it the seventh state without a capital punishment law.

A raid on a London top-security prison frees British train robber.

Nine people are indicted in New York for conspiring to arrange student tour of Cuba.

YOU USE THIS FOR BAKING???

U.S. narcotics agents arrest three alleged heroin smugglers, including the Mexican ambassador to Bolivia, in New York.

In conducting a search for gambling tax violators, at least 100 people are arrested by IRS agents in a nationwide raid.

SOMETIMES YOU SHOULD BE YOUR SISTER'S KEEPER

New York City police reveal a shocking fact that 28-year-old Kitty Genovese was stabbed to death as her neighbors stared through windows and did nothing to come to her rescue.

SEARCHING FOR THE ONE-ARMED MAN

Calling his trial "a mockery of justice," a Ohio Federal District judge orders the release of **Dr. Samuel H. Sheppard**, convicted of murdering his wife.

THE END OF A REIGN OF TERROR

Albert DeSalvo, thought to be the Boston Strangler, a modern-day Jack the Ripper, is arrested and confesses to hundreds of assaults against women.

Albert DeSalvo

HE'S SINGING LIKE A BOID

Mafioso-turned-informant **Joseph Valachi** writes his autobiography entitled THE REAL THING while in protective custody in a Washington, D.C. jail.

A mistrial is declared in the perjury trial of **Roy M. Cohn** following a juror being excused due to a death in the family.

Roy M. Cohn

THIEVES THAT GO BUMP IN THE NIGHT

A rare jewel collection, including the world's largest sapphire, the Star of India, as well as the Lone Star Ruby and the Midnight Sapphire, is stolen from New York's American Museum of Natural History. A tip-off to the police leads to the arrest of three men, all in their 20's.

FINGER-LICKIN' GOOD

Rare stamps, with an estimated value of $500,000, are stolen from an English dealership, making it the largest stamp robbery in history.

O.K. — WHAT IF YOU'RE COLOR-BLIND?

The new San Francisco Hilton offers drive-in check-in service whereby guests register at the garage entrance, get their room keys by pneumatic tube and then drive up the ramp to search for their room, which is color coordinated to their key tab.

The Port of N.Y. Authority announces plans for building the world's tallest buildings, the 110-story twin towers of the **World Trade Center**, which will eclipse the Empire State Building's position as the tallest building in the world. It is believed that if the new techniques applied in constructing the World Trade Center prove economical, a new era of "super-skyscrapers" may be ushered into our cities.

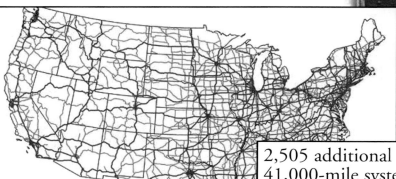

2,505 additional miles of the 41,000-mile system of interstate highways open to traffic at year-end.

BRIDGING THE GAPS

A BRIDGE NOT QUITE FAR ENOUGH

The world's longest bridge, a causeway over Lake Pontchartrain, north of New Orleans, is severed when two barges ram into it and six people die as their Continental Trailways bus plunges into the water.

New York Harbor's $325 million Verrazano Narrows Bridge, the longest suspension span in the world, serving as a link between Brooklyn and Staten Island, has its first car crossing.

Europe's first automobile tunnel through the Alps, the Great Saint Bernard Tunnel, opens.

Great Britain and France announce a joint decision to build a 32-mile railroad tunnel under the English Channel connecting Folkestone with Sangatte.

The Chesapeake Bay Bridge-Tunnel, a 17.6-mile bridge-tunnel across the entrance to Chesapeake Bay, opens after four years of construction.

President Lyndon B. Johnson officiates at ground-breaking ceremonies at Concord, California for a new test track to be used by the San Francisco Bay Area Rapid Transit District (BART), with the first four miles of subway between San Francisco and Berkeley.

WHAT A YEAR IT WAS!

SCHOOL DAYS, SCHOOL DAYS, GOOD OLD GOLDEN RULE DAYS

The U.S. Office of Education announces a record enrollment of 52,900,000 students in all schools and higher institutions of learning.

Elementary and secondary student enrollment nationwide: 41,500,000

NOT QUITE READY FOR CORPORATE DESKS

Of the 500,000 college students graduating this year, nearly 20% are expected to sign up for post-graduate studies.

Rising steadily over the last 13 years, college enrollment reaches an all-time record of 4,950,000 students.

THEY WON'T TAKE THIS STANDING UP

In the largest mass arrest in American history, 796 students are arrested at the University of California, Berkeley during demonstrations, including sit-ins, protesting the banning of student political activity on campus.

NUMBER OF YOUNGSTERS OFF TO SUMMER CAMP

Approximately 1,000,000 Off to 4,000 Private Camps

VIM & VIGOR *(An Exercise Plan for 18-Year-Olds)*

	BOYS	GIRLS
Sit-ups	80	50
Pull-ups	14	8
Swimming	880 yards	680 yards
Standing Broad Jump	8 ft. 6 in.	6 ft. 7 in.
Walking/Running	600 yards (one min., 30 sec.)	600 yards (two min., 30 sec.)

SCORE ONE FOR FREEDOM OF THE PRESS

The U.S. Supreme Court rules that a public official cannot win libel damages for criticism of his performance in office unless he can prove that a newspaper or magazine knows in advance that its statements are false or they are made with "reckless disregard."

A Florida ban against the sale of Henry Miller's autobiographical novel, TROPIC OF CANCER, is lifted when the U.S. Supreme Court rules that it is not legally obscene.

Bantam publishes a paperback edition of the WARREN COMMISSION REPORT within 80 hours of its release.

BAN IS LIFTED FASTER THAN A SPEEDING BULLET

Peru's Education Ministry ban on SUPERMAN and 14 other comics on the grounds that "their illogical and immoral actions contribute to unsettle children's imagination," is quickly lifted as protests grow and accusations of censorship are hurled.

U.S. HOLDS #1 POSITION IN WORLDWIDE NUMBER OF DAILY NEWSPAPERS

U.S.	1,758
Germany	473

WHAT A CONCEPT! THE TRUTH, NOTHING BUT THE TRUTH!

The LOS ANGELES FREE PRESS is founded, paving the way for a wave of underground newspapers.

THE WIZARD OF ID makes its comic strip debut.

WHAT A YEAR IT WAS!

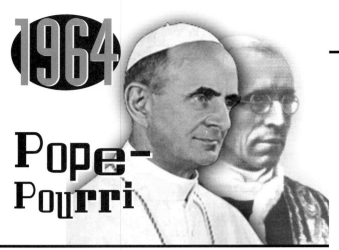

1964

Pope-Pourri

Pope Paul VI   *Pope Pius XII*

• Nazi documents made public assert that Pope Pius XII was an Axis sympathizer during World War II.

• Pope Paul VI announces his readiness to mediate in international disputes affecting peace.

• The Vatican abolishes Latin as the official language of Roman Catholic liturgy.

• The Vatican finally condemns anti-Semitism and warns against accusing the Jews of responsibility for the crucifixion of Christ.

• Pope Paul signs first encyclical calling for dialogue with non-Christians.

COMMUNION & CIGARETTES

Pope Paul VI is teary-eyed as 600 inmates of a Rome jail respond to his Mass, which he closes by announcing that each of them will receive two packs of cigarettes.

BELIEVERS SAY IT'S O.K. TO BE A NONBELIEVER

The executive committee of the World Council of Churches upholds the principle that all men have the right not only to have religious beliefs but also to be atheists.

IN GOD THEY DO NOT TRUST

According to the newspaper PRAVDA, the Soviet Communist Party's Central Committee has established a nationwide program to promote the abolition of religion in the Soviet Union and to encourage atheism.

The National Council of Churches representing 31 Protestant and Eastern Orthodox denominations condemns anti-Semitism and urges a dialogue with religious bodies of the Jewish community.

Rev. Frederick Richard McManus conducts the first mass in English in the United States at the opening of the 25th annual Liturgical Week in St. Louis.

FASTER THAN A SPEEDING...

Japan's Bullet electric train, designed to travel as fast as 159 mph, is off and running.

THEIR DREAM COULD COME TRUE

Hoping to dominate electronics in the future, Japan completes a revolutionary eight-mile monorail linking Tokyo and its airport.

First Minuteman II ICBM is tested in Florida.

Three Soviet astronauts land after orbiting the earth 16 times in 24 hours.

HELLO? IS THIS SUSHI TAKE-OUT?

The first underwater communications cable links Japan, the U.S. and Canada.

As a result of the new communication link, television viewers in North America see opening ceremonies of the Olympic Games from Tokyo via satellite and the U.S. military uses both satellite and cable for the first time as links with war-torn South Vietnam.

HOLD THE SALT

U.S. and Israel enter into discussions on joint research into using nuclear power to turn salt water into fresh water to solve Israel's irrigation problems.

Lying 192 feet on the ocean floor off the coast of Bermuda, *Sealab* is the first human habitat to be tested by the Naval Deep Submergence Systems Project.

WHAT A YEAR IT WAS!

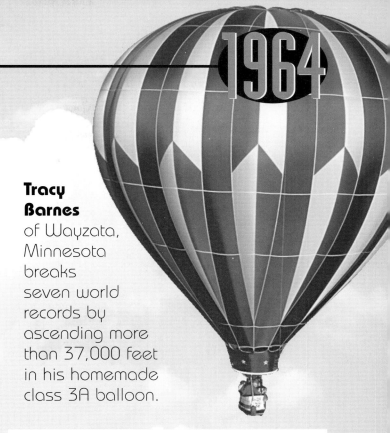

a woman's place is in the plane

Flying a Cessna-180, aviatrix **Geraldine Mock** becomes the first woman to complete solo flight around the world.

Encountering such obstacles as bad weather and a Brazilian revolution, following the same equatorial course pursued by the late Amelia Earhart on her fatal 1937 flight, California aviatrix **Joan Merriam Smith**, 27, flies around the globe in 56 days covering a total of 27,750 miles in a twin-engine Piper Apache.

Flying a needle-nosed F-104G Super Starfighter 37,000 feet above California's Edwards Air Force Base, aviatrix **Jacqueline Cochran** breaks her own record, setting the women's speed record of 1,429.2 mph, more than twice the speed of sound.

Tracy Barnes of Wayzata, Minnesota breaks seven world records by ascending more than 37,000 feet in his homemade class 3A balloon.

18TH ANNUAL **powder puff** DERBY WINNERS

Pilot: **Mary Ann Noah**
Co-Pilot: **Mary Aikins**

FEDERATION AERONAUTIQUE INTERNATIONALE GOLD MEDAL

Jacqueline Auriol of France
(Set the World Closed-Course Speed Record for Women - 1,266 mph)

HARMON INTERNATIONAL AVIATION TROPHIES

Mrs. Betty Miller
(Solo flight from Oakland, California to Sydney, Australia)

The new 2,000 mph B-70 bomber, capable of flying three times the speed of sound, makes its formal debut in Palmdale, California.

WHY? *BECAUSE IT'S THERE!*

A Japanese expedition, led by a Sherpa guide, scales the 25,910-foot Himalayan Peak Gyachung Kang.

A Chinese Communist team reaches the summit of the 26,291-foot Shishapangma on the Nepal-Tibet border.

Descending into the sea in the French bathy-scaphe *Archimede*, three men reach the deepest known spot in the Atlantic Ocean, the bottom of the 27,510-foot Puerto Rico Trench.

71-year-old American explorer and author, **William Willis**, crosses the Pacific Ocean on a raft named *Age Unlimited*.

Rear Admiral **James R. Reedy** leads U.S. Navy explorers in the discovery of a new mountain range and the world's longest glacier in the Antarctic.

BRING YOUR LONG JOHNS, BOYS

An international team, including 150 Americans, sets out on the first leg of a four-year expedition into what is the last unexplored region of Antarctica.

POPULAR AD CAMPAIGNS

Pepsi

AMERICAN VERSION
"Come Alive – You're in the Pepsi Generation"

GERMAN VERSION
"Come Alive Out of the Grave"

JAPANESE VERSION
"Pepsi Brings Your Ancestors Back from the Dead"

ESSO CARTOON TIGER
"Put a Tiger in Your Tank"

ALKA-SELTZER
"No Matter What Shape Your Stomach's In"

CLAIROL NICE 'n' EASY SHAMPOO-IN HAIR COLOR
"The Closer You Get...The Better You Look"

A Gallup Poll indicates that 63% of people interviewed say they drink alcoholic beverages.

HE'LL TAKE HIS MEDIUM DRY
A survey by a Chicago company reveals that 26% of men who drink martinis like theirs made with four parts gin to one part vermouth.

GOOD TO THE LAST DROP
The 62-nation Council of the International Coffee Organization breaks its dead-lock and agrees on a world coffee export quota of 48,006,518 bags for the year ending September 30, 1965.

AND NOW FOR YOUR VIEWING PLEASURE
American Airlines introduces movies on Astrovision.

The percentage of American families deficient in at least one major food group rose from 40% to 50% and is thought to be directly related to the huge 10-year growth in snack and convenience food sales.

A LAST – THE SMOKING GUN?
In response to the Surgeon General's report linking cigarette smoking to lung cancer and other diseases, the FTC plans to set severe limits on cigarette advertising and is proposing that warning messages be placed on cigarette packs and an end to endorsements by athletes.

ARE YOU MY DADDY?
Author **Pearl Buck** has founded Fathers Anonymous, an organization devoted to raising funds for children of American servicemen overseas.

Passings

Charles Graham, 111
The oldest former slave in the United States.

Bernice S. Pyke, 84
Women's suffragist and first woman delegate to a political convention.

Thomas Winston Briggs, 77
Creator of Welcome Wagon International, now with welcome wagons in over 2,000 cities.

WHAT A YEAR IT WAS!

New Words & Expressions

Nuke
An abbreviated name for a nuclear weapon.

Cryosurgery
When intense cold is used in surgery to remove tissue.

Appalachia
The part of the United States reaching from Alabama to Pennsylvania where poverty is rampant.

Quasar
Newly discovered, faraway celestial power source.

Cyberculture
The modern society that combines people with artificial, often automatic or electronic, entities.

Cyborg
A machine comprised of a mixture of organic and mechanical matter.

Solid Logic Technology
Computers that run faster yet are smaller than previous models.

Au Pair Girl
A foreign young woman who lives with a family while taking care of the children and the house.

Touch Tone Telephone
A telephone that uses pushbuttons in place of a dial.

Bang
The sonic roar heard when a plane reaches the speed of sound.

Demographic Edition
A magazine or other reading matter that is sent to customers favored by advertisers.

WASP
White Anglo-Saxon Protestant.

Brain Drain
The loss of many intelligent people.

Discotheque
A club for dancing.

Watusi
A popular dance with some similarities to the Twist.

Chimponaut
A chimpanzee used in the space program.

Good Samaritan Law
A law that prevents doctors, nurses or any individuals who offer assistance at the scene of an accident from getting sued by an injured party.

Isometrics
A type of exercise that incorporates different muscles.

Winkle-Picker
A shoe favored by teenagers that is slender with a narrow toe.

Kinetic Sculpture
Sculpture, such as a mobile, that moves.

The REAL thing for thirst

NEW IMPROVED DEEP-CHILL FLAVOR PROCESS

Squirt cools your thirst with the REAL refreshment of sun-ripened citrus. No artificial flavor or color. No excessive sweetness. Therefore, no after-thirst. And Squirt makes a marvelous mixer. No wonder.

FRESH, DRY FLAVOR FROM SUN-RIPENED CITRUS

60

Arts & ENTERTAINMENT

MOVIES

American films are growing more daring in their depiction of sex and provocative dialogue. Among the films that fall into that category are *A Shot in the Dark* and *The Americanization of Emily*.

Peter Sellers in A Shot in the Dark.

BEATLEMANIA!

MUSIC

The album *Meet the Beatles* is released in the U.S. on Capitol Records. It's the British group's U.S. debut LP.

Fans scream for the Fab Four.

TELEVISION

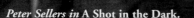
Clockwise from top: Barbara Parkins, Dorothy Malone, Ryan O'Neal

Described by **Jack Paar** as *"television's first situation orgy,"* the first nighttime soap opera, **Peyton Place**, starring **Mia Farrow** and **Ryan O'Neal**, draws an audience of approximately 60 million and is among the highest rated of the new programs.

ART

The U.N. building in New York receives a gift from **Marc Chagall**: a huge stained glass piece in honor of the late Secretary General of the U.N., **Dag Hammarskjöld**.

Chagall (left) and U.N. Secretary General U Thant

What's Playing AT THE MOVIES

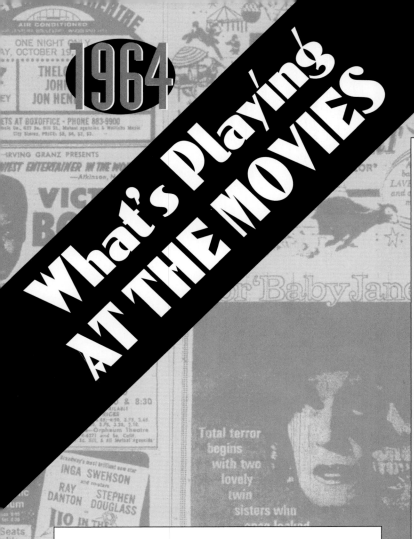

7 Faces Of Dr. Lao
A Fistful Of Dollars
A Hard Day's Night
A SHOT IN THE DARK
THE AMERICANIZATION OF EMILY
BECKET
BEDTIME STORY
Behold A Pale Horse
The Best Man
BLACK LIKE ME

THE CARETAKER
The Carpetbaggers
THE CHALK GARDEN
Cheyenne Autumn
THE COOL WORLD
DEAD RINGER
Dear Heart
DR. STRANGELOVE OR: HOW I LEARNED TO STOP WORRYING AND LOVE THE BOMB
The Empty Canvas
Fail-Safe
Fate Is The Hunter
FATHER GOOSE
For Those Who Think Young
Four Days In November
Girl With Green Eyes
Goldfinger
Good Neighbor Sam
Goodbye Charlie
HAMLET
Hey There, It's Yogi Bear

WHAT A YEAR IT WAS!

I'd Rather Be Rich

KISS ME, STUPID

Lady In A Cage

LILITH

THE LIVELY SET

The Long Ships

LORD JIM

Marnie

MARRIAGE ITALIAN STYLE

Mary Poppins

McHale's Navy

The Moon-Spinners

Muscle Beach Party

My Fair Lady

THE NIGHT OF THE IGUANA

Nothing But A Man

Nothing But The Best

One Potato, Two Potato

THE OUTRAGE

PAJAMA PARTY

PARIS WHEN IT SIZZLES

THE PATSY

THE PAWNBROKER

The Pink Panther

Ride The Wild Surf

Robin And The 7 Hoods

Robinson Crusoe On Mars

Séance On A Wet Afternoon

SEND ME NO FLOWERS

Seven Days In May

Sex And The Single Girl

THE SILENCE

The Soft Skin

Sunday In New York

SURF PARTY

That Man From Rio

The Thin Red Line

Topkapi

The Train

THE UNSINKABLE MOLLY BROWN

VIVA LAS VEGAS

What A Way To Go!

Where Love Has Gone

World Without Sun

ZORBA THE GREEK

1964

36th Annual Academy Awards

Night Of The Oscar®

For the 36th time, the world's entertainment capital recognizes the year's top artists and achievements with the bestowal of the coveted Oscars®.

Gregory Peck names **Patricia Neal** as Best Actress.

Annabella accepts for Patricia Neal, who is in London. It is a triumph for Miss Neal, who is awakened in the night to hear the good news.

Frank Sinatra announces the Best Picture winner, *Tom Jones*, directed by **Tony Richardson**.

David V. Picker accepts for Tony Richardson, who is also in England.

WHAT A YEAR IT WAS!

In a dramatic moment, **Anne Bancroft** names the Best Actor of the year—**Sidney Poitier**, the first black actor to win such a high award.

The announcement receives cheers from the audience.

Poitier accepts the coveted statue.

The winner is choked with emotion as he begins his acceptance speech:

*"Because it is a long journey
 to this moment, I am naturally indebted to countless numbers of people.
 For all of them, all I can say is, a very special thank-you."*

A jubilant Poitier is escorted off stage by Miss Bancroft.

WHAT A YEAR IT WAS!

The Academy Awards

"And The Winner Is..."

Oscars® Presented in 1964

BEST PICTURE
TOM JONES

BEST ACTOR
SIDNEY POITIER, *Lilies Of The Field*

BEST ACTRESS
PATRICIA NEAL, *Hud*

BEST DIRECTOR
TONY RICHARDSON, *Tom Jones*

BEST SUPPORTING ACTOR
MELVYN DOUGLAS, *Hud*

BEST SUPPORTING ACTRESS
MARGARET RUTHERFORD, *The VIPs*

BEST SONG
"CALL ME IRRESPONSIBLE," *Papa's Delicate Condition*

Sidney Poitier

1964 Favorites (Oscars® Presented in 1965)

BEST PICTURE
MY FAIR LADY

BEST ACTOR
REX HARRISON, *My Fair Lady*

BEST ACTRESS
JULIE ANDREWS, *Mary Poppins*

BEST DIRECTOR
GEORGE CUKOR, *My Fair Lady*

BEST SUPPORTING ACTOR
PETER USTINOV, *Topkapi*

BEST SUPPORTING ACTRESS
LILA KEDROVA, *Zorba The Greek*

BEST SONG
"CHIM CHIM CHER-EE," *Mary Poppins*

COSTUME DESIGN, COLOR
CECIL BEATON, *My Fair Lady*

Julie Andrews

WHAT A YEAR IT WAS!

Dame Edith Evans *Honored in New York*

LILLIAN GISH is among the impressive group of celebrities who gather in New York to honor **DAME EDITH EVANS.**

Her countryman, **SIR CEDRIC HARDWICKE,** is one of the guests *(right)* as well as perennial favorite **MYRNA LOY,** also here to pay tribute *(below).*

ALEXIS SMITH and **HOWARD KEEL** are honoring the British actress *(right),* along with **JANIS PAIGE** and **THELMA RITTER** *(below).*

SYBIL BURTON also aids in representing England.

Universal President **MILTON RACKMIL** *(left)* and **ROSS HUNTER,** producer of *The Chalk Garden,* join in the festivities.

Ross Hunter presents Dame Edith a token of his appreciation saying that he wants to make a personal acknowledgment of Dame Edith's outstanding work in *The Chalk Garden.*

WHAT A YEAR IT WAS!

STILL GORGEOUS AFTER ALL THESE YEARS

Cary Grant

Movie idol **Cary Grant** turns 60 and according to columnist **Sheilah Graham** women of all ages are still swooning.

In an interview while filming *Father Goose* with his considerably younger co-star **Leslie Caron**, **Cary Grant** says, "The public doesn't like to see an older man making love to a young girl. It offends them. And I must say I agree with them."

UNIVERSAL STUDIOS opens its doors to public tours.

The U.S. motion picture industry reports its biggest profits since television became its major competitor.

Edward G. Robinson replaces ailing **Spencer Tracy** in *Cheyenne Autumn*.

Bob Hope begins his 50th Hollywood movie.

Bob Hope

The Umbrellas of Cherbourg is one of the winners at the 17th annual Cannes Film Festival.

Despite the sizzling 90 degree heat in Manhattan, 2,500 people, including **Elizabeth Taylor**, **Richard Burton** and **Ava Gardner**, turn out for the $100-a-seat premiere of *The Night of the Iguana*.

HE NEEDS TO "WATCH" HIMSELF

With Swedish actress **Britt Ekland** at his side, 38-year-old **Peter Sellers** leaves a Los Angeles hospital where he is rushed after suffering an almost fatal heart attack.

John Wayne is in intensive care at Los Angeles' Good Samaritan Hospital where he is recovering from the removal of a lung abscess.

While filming *None but the Brave* in Hawaii, **Frank Sinatra** is rescued from an undertow while swimming in Wailua Bay, Kauai.

Frank Sinatra

THE BLUE PENCIL IS PUT AWAY

The U.S. Supreme Court reverses a Cleveland Heights ban on the French movie *The Lovers*.

HASTY PUDDING WOMAN OF THE YEAR
Rosalind Russell

WHAT A YEAR IT WAS!

PASSINGS

Eddie Cantor, 72

Star of vaudeville, Broadway, radio, motion pictures and television, Cantor is renowned for his blackface, singing, dancing, joking and philanthropy. The former president of the Screen Actors Guild, Cantor coined the phrase "March of Dimes" and suggested people send their dimes to White House polio victim, President Franklin Delano Roosevelt, to help find a cure.

Sir Cedric Hardwicke, 71

One of the greatest character actors in the early years of cinema, Hardwicke first became famous on the British stage. American movie audiences know him best from *The Winslow Boy, A Connecticut Yankee in King Arthur's Court* and *The Ten Commandments.*

Alan Ladd, 50

Handsome motion picture star who is best remembered for his gunfighter role in *Shane.*

Peter Lorre, 59

The infamous bad guy of films, Lorre is remembered for his roles in *M, Casablanca, The Maltese Falcon* and *Crime and Punishment.*

Harpo Marx, 75

The non-speaking, harp-playing, wig-wearing, pantomime master of the Marx Brothers comedy team. Harpo and his brothers started in vaudeville, moved on to Broadway, and eventually made many films, including *A Day at the Races, A Night at the Opera, Duck Soup* and *Love Happy.*

Harpo Marx

Famous BIRTHS

Juliette Binoche
Sandra Bullock
Nicolas Cage
Cedric the Entertainer
Don Cheadle
Russell Crowe
Hope Davis
Matt Dillon
Bridget Fonda
Vivica A. Fox
Janeane Garofalo
Bonnie Hunt
John Leguizamo
Laura Linney
Mary-Louise Parker
Keanu Reeves
David Spade
Marisa Tomei

TOP MONEYMAKER OF THE YEAR
THE CARPETBAGGERS

SAMUEL BRONSTON presents

SOPHIA LOREN
STEPHEN BOYD / ALEC GUINNESS
JAMES MASON / CHRISTOPHER PLUMMER

THE FALL OF THE ROMAN EMPIRE

co-starring
JOHN IRELAND / MEL FERRER / OMAR SHARIF
ANTHONY QUAYLE

Original Screenplay by BEN BARZMAN · BASILIO FRANCHINA · PHILIP YORDAN · Produced by SAMUEL BRONSTON
Directed by ANTHONY MANN | Music by DIMITRI TIOMKIN
ULTRA-PANAVISION · TECHNICOLOR · A Paramount Release

FLOP OF THE YEAR
THE FALL OF THE ROMAN EMPIRE

MOST EXPENSIVE FILM OF THE YEAR
MY FAIR LADY ($17,000,000)

NEW YORK CRITICS AWARD

MOTION PICTURE	*MY FAIR LADY*
ACTOR	Rex Harrison *MY FAIR LADY*
ACTRESS	Kim Stanley *SÉANCE ON A WET AFTERNOON*
DIRECTOR	Stanley Kubrick *DR. STRANGELOVE*
FOREIGN FILM	*THAT MAN FROM RIO*

WHAT A YEAR IT WAS!

BIG BUCKS AT THE
BOX OFFICE

Jerry Lewis

Ann-Margret
Doris Day
Cary Grant
Rock Hudson
Jack Lemmon
Jerry Lewis
Shirley MacLaine
Paul Newman
Elvis Presley
John Wayne

Doris Day

STARS
OF TOMORROW

Elizabeth Ashley
Keir Dullea
Annette Funicello
Joey Heatherton
Dean Jones
Stefanie Powers
Harve Presnell
Nancy Sinatra
Elke Sommer
Susannah York

*John
Wayne*

Shirley MacLaine

*Rock
Hudson*

*Joey
Heatherton*

*Ann-
Margret*

New 13-inch Playmate

Only from Admiral. The new 13-inch Playmate
(overall diagonal)
gives you the Big Picture in personal portables. It has 30% more
picture area than the popular Admiral Playmate 11. <u>Yet the
cabinet size is the same!</u> Perfectly personal. Rugged, light.
It's the most powerful personal portable made . . . with
82-channel tuning at no extra cost.

There's nothing finer at any price, so . . .

take two, they're small!

$99.95* buys a precision-quality Playmate 11.
New Playmate 13 from just $10 more!

Admiral®
MARK OF QUALITY THROUGHOUT THE WORLD

Shown above, Admiral Playmates, PD1310 Series. Private listening jack, telescopic monopole antenna. Two-tone styling in black, white, red or sandalwood-brown; all with golden-finish trim.
*Mfr. suggested list price. Slightly higher in some areas. Specifications subject to change without notice. Admiral, Chicago. Canadian Admiral, Port Credit, Ont.

72

TELEVISION 1964

What's Playing On TV

The Adventures Of Ozzie & Harriet

The Alfred Hitchcock Hour

The Andy Griffith Show

The Andy Williams Show

The Bell Telephone Hour

Ben Casey

The Beverly Hillbillies

The Bill Dana Show

Bob Hope Presents The Chrysler Theatre

Bonanza

Burke's Law

Candid Camera

Combat

The Danny Kaye Show

The Danny Thomas Show

Death Valley Days

The Defenders

The Dick Van Dyke Show

Dr. Kildare

The Ed Sullivan Show

The Farmer's Daughter

The Flintstones

Gunsmoke

Hazel

I've Got A Secret

The Jack Benny Program

The Jack Paar Program

Jackie Gleason And His American Scene Magazine

Lassie

The Lawrence Welk Show

The Lucy Show

McHale's Navy

Meet The Press

Mister Ed

Mr. Novak

My Favorite Martian

My Three Sons

The Nurses

The Outer Limits

Password

The Patty Duke Show

Petticoat Junction

The Price Is Right

Rawhide

The Red Skelton Show

Sing Along With Mitch

To Tell The Truth

The Twentieth Century

The Twilight Zone

The Virginian

Wagon Train

Walt Disney's Wonderful World Of Color

What's My Line?

NUMBER OF TV STATIONS WORLDWIDE
4,200

FACES ON THE BOOB TUBE

Bill Bixby

Sid Caesar

Don Adams
Edie Adams
Jack Albertson
Alan Alda
Don Ameche
Morey Amsterdam
James Arness
Edward Asner
John Astin
Jim Backus
Ralph Bellamy
Bill Bixby
Richard Boone
Shirley Booth
Tom Bosley
Charles Boyer
Walter Brennan
Beau Bridges
Charles Bronson
Ernest Borgnine
Art Buchwald
Carol Burnett
George Burns
Sid Caesar
Judy Carne
Leo G. Carroll
Pat Carroll
Richard Chamberlain
Imogene Coca
Chuck Connors
Tim Conway

Jackie Coogan
Joseph Cotten
Richard Crenna
Walter Cronkite
Bob Denver
Richard Dreyfuss
Clint Eastwood
Buddy Ebsen
Mia Farrow
Joe Flynn
William Frawley
Judy Garland
Ben Gazzara
Alice Ghostley
Lorne Greene
Fred Gwynne
Ron Howard
Jack Klugman
Don Knotts
Michael Landon
June Lockhart
Tina Louise
Allen Ludden
Gavin MacLeod
Fred MacMurray
Dorothy Malone
Rose Marie
E.G. Marshall
Burgess Meredith
Martin Milner
Elizabeth Montgomery

Joseph Cotten

June Lockhart

WHAT A YEAR IT WAS!

Mary Tyler Moore
Ken Murray
Jim Nabors
Bob Newhart
Julie Newmar
David Niven
Ryan O'Neal
The Osmond Brothers
Jack Palance
Fess Parker
Robert Reed
Carl Reiner
Burt Reynolds
Mickey Rooney
Marion Ross
Kurt Russell
George C. Scott
Rod Serling
Phil Silvers
Connie Stevens
Cicely Tyson
Rudy Vallee
Vivian Vance
Ray Walston
Dennis Weaver
Efrem Zimbalist Jr.

Ray Walston

Buddy Ebsen

Elizabeth Montgomery

YOU, TOO, CAN HAVE FUN WITH YOUR NEUROSIS

Comedian **Woody Allen** is slated to take over as the first of **Johnny Carson's** vacation replacements on "The Tonight Show."

FAMOUS BIRTHS

Hank Azaria
Michael Boatman
Amy Brenneman
Courteney Cox
David Eigenberg
Chris Farley
Calista Flockhart
Faith Ford
Melissa Gilbert
Jasmine Guy
Mariska Hargitay
Teri Hatcher
Rob Lowe
Gloria Reuben
Caroline Rhea
French Stewart
Wanda Sykes
Blair Underwood

NEW SHOWS On The TV BLOCK
(A Sampling)

GONE FOREVER

ABC Scope
The Addams Family
Another World
Bewitched
The Bing Crosby Show
Broadside
The Cara Williams
    Show
The Celebrity Game
Daniel Boone
The Entertainers
The Famous Adventures
    Of Mr. Magoo
Flipper

Gilligan's Island
Gomer Pyle, U.S.M.C.
The Hollywood Palace
Jeopardy!
Jonny Quest
The Magilla Gorilla
    Show
The Man From
    U.N.C.L.E.
Many Happy Returns
Mickey
Mr. Broadway
The Munsters
My Living Doll
Peyton Place
The Reporter
Shindig!
Slattery's People
That Was The Week
    That Was
Twelve O'Clock High
Voyage To The Bottom
    Of The Sea

Brenner
The Eleventh Hour
Empire
Hootenanny
Route 66
77 Sunset Strip

*The cast of 77 Sunset Strip, from left:
Efrem Zimbalist Jr., Edd "Kookie" Byrnes,
Roger Smith*

Shindig's
Bobby Sherman

AND NOW, FOR A REALLY GOOD CONTRACT

62-year-old **Ed Sullivan** is given a lifetime contract by CBS.

AND AWAY HE GOES

CBS-TV offers **Jackie Gleason** $6,000,000, the biggest one-year contract in the history of television, to entice him into one more season.

A FRIENDLY TAKEOVER

Richard S. Salant, president of CBS News, is replaced by producer **Fred W. Friendly**.

📺 The FCC renounces any right to censor sexually or politically provocative radio or television programs that may offend some listeners.

📺 The FCC holds hearings to decide whether or not it will authorize stereophonic sound for television.

📺 Pictures of the opening day ceremonies at the Olympic Games in Tokyo are transmitted through the satellite *Syncom III.*

📺 **The Supremes** make their first appearance on "The Ed Sullivan Show."

📺 Addressing University of North Carolina students, **David Brinkley** quips: "Television is the only thing in the world that is punctual. It may be lousy, but it's on time."

📺 California's experiment in pay television suffers a setback when the state's voters approve an amendment outlawing Pay TV in that state.

EQUAL OPPORTUNITY TO BLAH-BLAH

A bill suspending the requirement that broadcasters provide equal time for all legally qualified candidates in an election is killed by the Senate, 44-41.

The two major political parties spend a record $40,000,000 on television ads, and election night returns are computed and analyzed with record speed by the three big networks, which accurately predict the Democratic victory before 9:30 p.m.

EXIT THE EXIT POLLS?

With regard to national elections, television executive and former press secretary for Dwight D. Eisenhower, James C. Hagerty, suggests a national deadline before which no returns could be made public or simultaneous closing of polls in all states except Alaska and Hawaii.

1964 EMMY awards

Dick Van Dyke and Mary Tyler Moore

SERIES

Comedy
The Dick Van Dyke Show

Drama
The Defenders

Variety
The Danny Kaye Show

Program Of The Year
The Making of the President 1960

ENTERTAINERS

Actor | **Dick Van Dyke** *The Dick Van Dyke Show*

Actress | **Mary Tyler Moore** *The Dick Van Dyke Show*

Performer (Variety or Musical) | **Danny Kaye** *The Danny Kaye Show*

Comedy Writing | **Carl Reiner** *The Dick Van Dyke Show*

Danny Kaye

Promoting the first prime-time lineup to offer more than half the shows in color, NBC launches its fall schedule in a single week, following the strategy ABC used last year.

PASSINGS

Gracie Allen, age unknown
For over three decades, she was the Allen in the Burns & Allen comedy team. They performed in vaudeville, motion pictures, radio and television. The ditsy part of the duo, Allen's famous line, "Say goodnight, Gracie," is a beloved part of entertainment history. Allen, a native of San Francisco, lost her birth certificate in the 1906 earthquake, so her exact age is not known.

William Bendix, 58
The star of *The Life of Riley* on radio, television and in the movies. The show was on television for eight seasons.

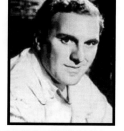

WHAT A YEAR IT WAS!

DER BINGLE'S SPONSOR GOES UP IN SMOKE

OLD POPULAR RADIO PROGRAMS RETURN

THE SHADOW

Inner Sanctum Mysteries

The Green Hornet

The Lone Ranger

NUMBER OF RADIO STATIONS WORLDWIDE 10,514

Radio is the nation's second most utilized communications medium, with newspapers ranking first and television third.

A spokesman for **BING CROSBY** announces that Bing has declined sponsorship of his radio program by the Liggett & Myers Tobacco Co., makers of Chesterfield, L&M and Lark cigarettes.

N ew York radio station WMCA drops all cigarette commercials from a daily four-hour disc jockey show aimed at teenagers.

D espite protests by the Distilled Spirits Institute, *N.Y. Times*-owned radio station WQXR announces it will accept whiskey advertising.

RADIO

From breakfast to bedtime

extension phones work hard for you day and night, save steps and
time, give comfort, privacy and protection. You can choose yours in
decorator colors; just call the Business Office or ask your telephone man.

 Bell System

American Telephone & Telegraph Co. and Associated Companies

80

POPULAR MUSIC

1964

The Beatles *make their first appearance on "The Ed Sullivan Show" drawing 73 million people, the largest U.S. television audience in history.*

BEATLEMANIA!

The Beatles play two concerts at New York City's Carnegie Hall.

For the first time, *BILLBOARD* lists one act, the Beatles, with five songs in the Hot 100.

The Beatles start working on their first feature-length movie, *A Hard Day's Night.*

The Beatles' *I Want to Hold Your Hand* and *She Loves You* are, according to *BILLBOARD*, "neck and neck" for the top spot on the singles chart.

BILLBOARD reports Beatles records have claimed 60% of the singles market.

Can't Buy Me Love debuts at No. 1 on the charts.

The Beatles hold the top five positions on *BILLBOARD'S* Hot 100 as follows: 1. *Can't Buy Me Love,* 2. *Twist and Shout,* 3. *She Loves You,* 4. *I Want to Hold Your Hand,* 5. *Please, Please Me.*

The Beatles' *Second Album* reaches No. 1 on the U.S. LP charts in its second week of release—the first album ever to make it to the top that quickly.

Beatles manager **Brian Epstein** claims the group's U.S. tour (August 19-September 20) is a sellout.

Beatles beach towel, flag, Halloween costume, pillow.

THE BEATLES INVADE AMERICA

3,000

screaming teenagers overwhelm Kennedy Airport to greet the Beatles, Liverpool's John Lennon, 23; Paul McCartney, 21; George Harrison, 21; and Ringo Starr, 23, whose recording of *I Want to Hold Your Hand* has skyrocketed to Number 1 on this side of the Atlantic.

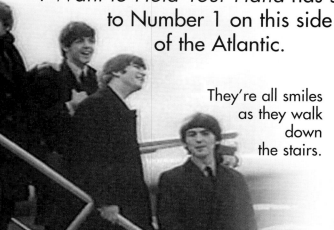

They're all smiles as they walk down the stairs.

Their first meeting with the American press brings forth an interview laced with quips and humor. Their popularity has risen steadily in Europe where they have reached the peak of pop stardom, resulting in a gross of $17 million last year. Their recording of *Can't Buy Me Love* has resulted in 2.1 million orders, an all-time high for a single.

The pandemonium follows the musicians into Manhattan, where a huge number of teenyboppers gather outside the Plaza Hotel waving welcome signs.

The signs are reminiscent of the hero worship in the heydays of Elvis Presley and Frank Sinatra.

ELVIS IS DEAD. EVER LONG LIVE US THE BEATLES

New York City cops are on hand to protect the Beatles from their hysterical fans.

WHAT A YEAR IT WAS!

With Beatle George in bed with a sore throat, three of the quartet leave the hotel to take an airing in Central Park.

Photographers are on hand in Central Park to catch their antics.

All joking aside, the Beatles have a heavy schedule ahead of them and are scheduled to appear live on "The Ed Sullivan Show" and perform two sold-out shows at Carnegie Hall. It appears that "Beatlemania" has officially invaded America.

WHAT A YEAR IT WAS!

The film *A Hard Day's Night* premieres in the Beatles' hometown of Liverpool. Hundreds of thousands line the streets from the airport to the city center for a parade.

A *Hard Day's Night* opens to mixed reviews ranging from "avoid this film at all costs" to "amusing and engaging."

The Beatles' first U.S. tour opens at the Cow Palace in San Francisco on a bill including **Jackie DeShannon** and the **Righteous Brothers**.

Liberty Records reports that the album *The Chipmunks Sing the Beatles* is selling 25,000 copies a day.

The Beatles play the first of two concerts at New York's Forest Hills Tennis Stadium. 15,000 attend each performance and show their affection by tossing jelly beans, the band's favorite candy, onto the stage. The fans scream so loud, it's almost impossible to hear the music.

Beatle George Harrison forms his own song publishing company, Harrissongs.

At Cleveland's Public Auditorium, the Beatles are ordered off the stage by authorities for 15 minutes so that the screaming crowd can calm down.

The Beatles perform a charity show in Brooklyn, New York to finish their U.S. tour. Later that night they appear on "The Ed Sullivan Show."

Beatles manager **Brian Epstein** turns down a $3 1/2 million offer from a group of U.S. businessmen to buy out his management contract.

The Beatles appear on an episode of "Shindig!" taped on location in London. They perform *I'm a Loser, Kansas City* and *Boys*.

George Harrison's girlfriend **Patti Boyd** is attacked by female Beatle fans at one of the group's Christmas shows in London. It seems the fans were resentful of Patti's place in George Harrison's life.

Beatles drummer **Ringo Starr** checks into London's University College Hospital to have his tonsils removed.

POPULAR SONGS

A Hard Day's Night
The Beatles

Come A Little Bit Closer
Jay & The Americans

I Want To Hold Your Hand
The Beatles

A World Without Love
Peter & Gordon

Dancing In The Street
Martha & The Vandellas

Glad All Over
The Dave Clark Five

House Of The Rising Sun
The Animals

I'm Gonna Be Strong
Gene Pitney

And I Love Her
The Beatles

Dang Me
Roger Miller

Goin' Out Of My Head
Little Anthony & The Imperials

How Sweet It Is To Be Loved By You
Marvin Gaye

I'm Into Something Good
Herman's Hermits

Baby Love
The Supremes

Don't Let The Sun Catch You Crying
Gerry & The Pacemakers

Hello, Dolly!
Louis Armstrong

I Feel Fine
The Beatles

It's All Over Now
The Rolling Stones

Baby, I Need Your Loving
Four Tops

Downtown
Petula Clark

High Heel Sneakers
Tommy Tucker

I Get Around
The Beach Boys

It's Over
Roy Orbison

The Animals

Can't Buy Me Love
The Beatles

Everybody Loves Somebody
Dean Martin

Leader Of The Pack
The Shangri-Las

Chapel Of Love
The Dixie Cups

Let It Be Me
Betty Everett & Jerry Butler

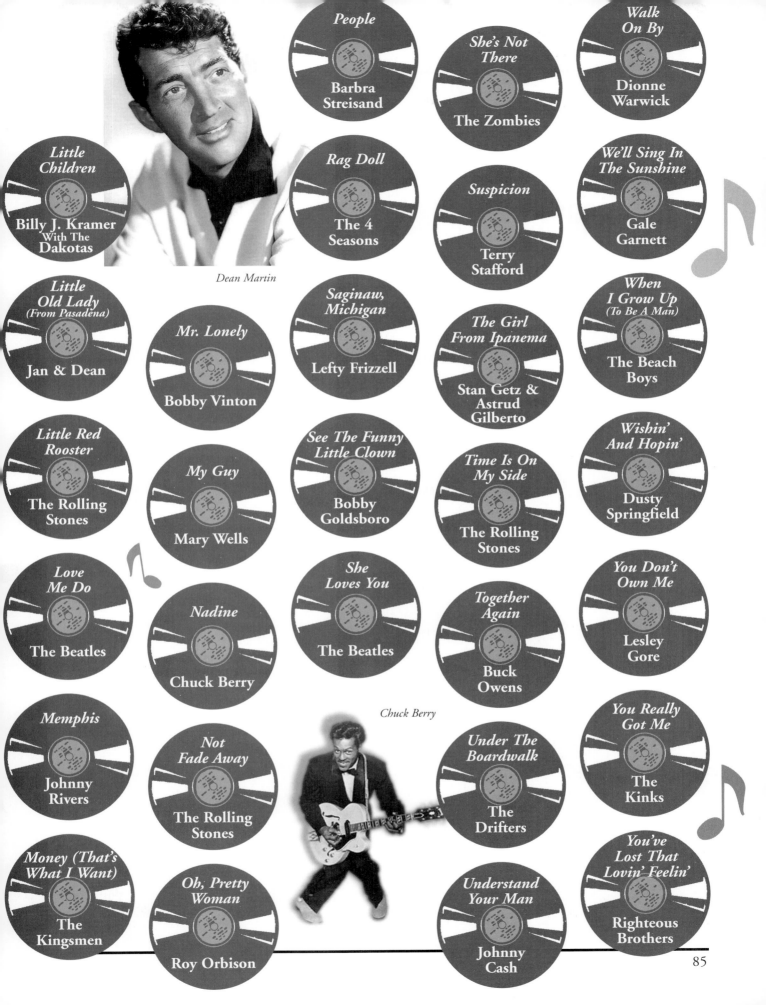

People — Barbra Streisand

She's Not There — The Zombies

Walk On By — Dionne Warwick

Little Children — Billy J. Kramer With The Dakotas

Dean Martin

Rag Doll — The 4 Seasons

Suspicion — Terry Stafford

We'll Sing In The Sunshine — Gale Garnett

Little Old Lady (From Pasadena) — Jan & Dean

Mr. Lonely — Bobby Vinton

Saginaw, Michigan — Lefty Frizzell

The Girl From Ipanema — Stan Getz & Astrud Gilberto

When I Grow Up (To Be A Man) — The Beach Boys

Little Red Rooster — The Rolling Stones

My Guy — Mary Wells

See The Funny Little Clown — Bobby Goldsboro

Time Is On My Side — The Rolling Stones

Wishin' And Hopin' — Dusty Springfield

Love Me Do — The Beatles

Nadine — Chuck Berry

She Loves You — The Beatles

Together Again — Buck Owens

You Don't Own Me — Lesley Gore

Chuck Berry

Memphis — Johnny Rivers

Not Fade Away — The Rolling Stones

Under The Boardwalk — The Drifters

You Really Got Me — The Kinks

Money (That's What I Want) — The Kingsmen

Oh, Pretty Woman — Roy Orbison

Understand Your Man — Johnny Cash

You've Lost That Lovin' Feelin' — Righteous Brothers

85

1964

BEST-SELLING FILM SOUNDTRACK ALBUMS

Mary Poppins
My Fair Lady
A Hard Day's Night

NEW RECORDING ARTISTS

The Animals
The Dave Clark Five
Petula Clark
Herman's Hermits
Al Hirt
Roger Miller
Peter & Gordon
Johnny Rivers
The Rolling Stones
Dusty Springfield
The Temptations

GOLD RECORDS

The Beatles
Nat King Cole
The Kingston Trio
Al Hirt
Robert Russell Bennett
The 4 Seasons

• The Rolling Stones' debut album, *The Rolling Stones*, is released in the U.K. on Decca Records.

• The Rolling Stones arrive in New York to begin their first U.S. tour. Their first gig was at a high school stadium near Boston.

• The Rolling Stones meet two of their idols during a recording session as they run into bluesmen **Willie Dixon** and **Muddy Waters** at Chicago's Chess studios.

• The Rolling Stones begin their first headlining British tour in Harrow.

• The Rolling Stones appear as judges on the British "rate-a-record" TV show, "Juke Box Jury."

• The Rolling Stones make a television appearance on "Hollywood Palace."

• The Rolling Stones announce the cancellation of a planned South African tour due to an anti-apartheid embargo by the British Musicians' Union.

• The Rolling Stones make their first appearance on "The Ed Sullivan Show."

• The Rolling Stones show up late for the BBC radio shows "Top Gear" and "Saturday Club" and are banned by the BBC.

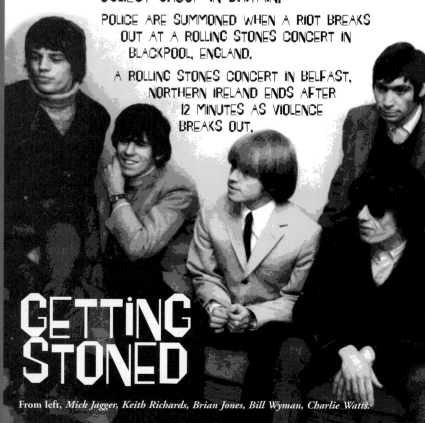

THE DAILY MIRROR CALLS THE ROLLING STONES THE UGLIEST GROUP IN BRITAIN.

POLICE ARE SUMMONED WHEN A RIOT BREAKS OUT AT A ROLLING STONES CONCERT IN BLACKPOOL, ENGLAND.

A ROLLING STONES CONCERT IN BELFAST, NORTHERN IRELAND ENDS AFTER 12 MINUTES AS VIOLENCE BREAKS OUT.

GETTING STONED

From left, *Mick Jagger, Keith Richards, Brian Jones, Bill Wyman, Charlie Watts.*

WHAT A YEAR IT WAS!

GRAMMY awards

Record of the Year
THE GIRL FROM IPANEMA
Stan Getz & Astrud Gilberto

Song of the Year
HELLO, DOLLY!
Jerry Herman, songwriter

Album of the Year
GETZ/GILBERTO
Stan Getz & Joao Gilberto

Vocal Performance, Female
PEOPLE
Barbra Streisand

Vocal Performance, Male
HELLO, DOLLY!
Louis Armstrong

Vocal Performance, Group
A HARD DAY'S NIGHT
The Beatles

Rock & Roll Recording
DOWNTOWN
Petula Clark

Folk Recording
WE'LL SING IN THE SUNSHINE
Gale Garnett

Instrumental Composition
THE PINK PANTHER THEME
Henry Mancini, composer

Original Cast Show Album
FUNNY GIRL

Original Score
MARY POPPINS

Comedy Performance
I STARTED OUT AS A CHILD
Bill Cosby

LOUIS ARMSTRONG'S recording of *Hello, Dolly!* is the first show tune to top the popular music charts in almost a decade.

27-year-old **SHIRLEY BASSEY** gets international attention with her recording of *Goldfinger* from the James Bond film.

JUDY GARLAND and **LIZA MINNELLI** give a mother-daughter concert in London.

BARBRA STREISAND makes the April 10th cover of *TIME*.

THE LITTLE SPARROW LIVES
Workmen find a box of 45 masters in the cellars of the Paris offices of Philips record company which were recorded by the late **EDITH PIAF** between 1940 and 1942.

AND THE MELODIES LINGER ON
Lyricist **IRA GERSHWIN** releases 17 unpublished compositions of his late brother, **GEORGE**, 14 of which are sent to **GEORGE BALANCHINE** of the N.Y. City Ballet for possible ballet use and the remaining three to be used by director **BILLY WILDER** in his upcoming film *Kiss Me, Stupid*.

ASCAP celebrates its Golden Anniversary.

The 63-year-old composer of *My Fair Lady*, Viennese-born **FREDERICK LOEWE**, bequeaths $1 million in royalties from *The Rain in Spain* to the Desert Hospital in Palm Springs, his adopted home.

STILL SINGING THE BLUES
Blues singer **MISSISSIPPI JOHN HURT** is rediscovered in Avalon, Mississippi and at age 72 he goes on the nightclub circuit for the first time with performances scheduled in Washington and New York.

Japan becomes a new center for jazz artists with **DUKE ELLINGTON**, **HARRY JAMES**, **COUNT BASIE**, **GERRY MILLIGAN** and **OSCAR PETERSON** among the more than 30 well-known leaders who are welcomed by Japanese fans.

Duke Ellington

Louis Armstrong

Count Basie

Mississippi John Hurt

Liza Minnelli

A SHATTERING EXPERIENCE
Singer **Kate** *"God Bless America"* **Smith** is in Good Samaritan Hospital in West Palm Beach, Florida with 25 stitches in her arm as a result of falling through a glass shower door.

Singer **Vic Damone** crashes his brand new Ferrari in the High Sierras only five hours after he purchased it for $15,000.

Jazzman and guitarist **Eddie Condon** is recovering in New York from prostate surgery.

Famous BIRTHS

Tracy Chapman
Wynonna Judd
Diana Krall
Lenny Kravitz
Maria McKee
Dave Pirner
Amy Ray
Eddie Vedder
CeCe Winans
Trisha Yearwood

Indiana **GOVERNOR WELSH** declares the song *Louie Louie* by the **KINGSMEN** (currently No. 6 on the Hot 100) pornographic.

Capitol Records is besieged with requests for heavyweight boxing champ **CASSIUS CLAY'S** album, *I Am the Greatest*.

ALAN FREED, the ex-DJ who helped put rock & roll on the musical map, is charged with tax evasion, the grand jury indictment stemming from the earlier payola investigation that ruined his career.

BOB DYLAN makes his first entry into the U.K. pop chart with *The Times They Are A-Changin'*.

THE MOODY BLUES are formed in Birmingham, England.

ROY ORBISON'S *Oh, Pretty Woman* hits No. 1 on the singles chart.

Downtown is the first U.S. hit by British pop singer **PETULA CLARK**.

THE ANIMALS put an electric sound to folk music and create folk-rock with their No. 1 hit, *House of the Rising Sun*.

SONGS, YES—GUNS, NO
Folk singer **JOAN BAEZ** takes on the IRS with regard to why she withheld 60% of her 1963 income taxes so they would not be used for armaments.

California surf-rock band **THE BEACH BOYS** make their first appearance on "The Ed Sullivan Show."

Beach Boys leader Brian Wilson suffers a nervous breakdown on a flight from L.A. to Houston, which leads him to stop touring with the group. Glen Campbell fills in for six months.

Passings

Sam Cooke, 33
Popular rock & roll singer whose many hits include "You Send Me," "Cousin of Mine," "Only Sixteen" and "Wonderful World."

Meade "Lux" Lewis, 58
Outstanding boogie-woogie and jazz pianist.

Jack Teagarden, 58
Blues- and jazz-playing Teagarden's trombone and voice were popular in New York in the 1920s. He later played with Louis Armstrong, Paul Whiteman, formed his own band and toured Asia under the auspices of the U.S. State Department.

Joan Baez

Alan Freed

Bob Dylan

Jack Teagarden

WHAT A YEAR IT WAS!

Classical Music

New Compositions & Operas

Curlew River
Benjamin Britten

~

Parole di San Paola
Luigi Dallapiccola

~

Montezuma
Roger Sessions
(composed in 1947, but
performed for the first time this year)

~

Symphony No. 10 (posth.)
Gustav Mahler
(completed by Deryck Cooke)

~

Plus-Minus
Karlheinz Stockhausen

~

The Last Savage
Gian Carlo Menotti
(American premiere)

BEST-SELLING CLASSICAL ALBUMS

Madama Butterfly
Leontyne Price

Carmen
Leontyne Price

Symphony No. 3 (Kaddish)
Leonard Bernstein

Piano Concerto No. 4 (Beethoven)
Van Cliburn

Verdi Arias
Maria Callas

Gian Carlo Menotti

Benjamin Britten

NEW YORK MUSIC CRITICS' CIRCLE AWARD

Operatic
A MIDSUMMER NIGHT'S DREAM
Benjamin Britten

•

Choral
WAR REQUIEM
Benjamin Britten

U.S. symphonies this year amount to 1,200—more than half the 2,000 symphonies worldwide.

NO PULITZER PRIZE IS GIVEN FOR MUSIC THIS YEAR.

WHAT A YEAR IT WAS!

SINGING THROUGH THE BARRIERS

Leontyne Price

Black Metropolitan Opera singer **LEONTYNE PRICE** gets a standing ovation from the 95% white audience following her performance in Atlanta of Mozart's *Don Giovanni*.

CAN THIS LITTLE GIRL FROM MISSISSIPPI...

37-year-old soprano **LEONTYNE PRICE**, on tour with Milan's La Scala Company, performs in Verdi's *Requiem* at Moscow's Bolshoi Theater and receives thunderous applause for 26 minutes that includes 16 curtain calls.

SITTING DOWN ON THE JOB

Conductor **Pierre Monteux** falls through a guardrail on the podium in Rome's Santa Cecilia Auditorium where he is conducting **Ravel's** *Pavan for a Dead Princess*. Regaining consciousness, the maestro insists on finishing the concert and conducts the balance of the program sitting in a chair.

At intermission, about one-third of the subscription audience walks out on **John Cage's** avant-garde *Atlas Eclipticalis with Winter Music*.

Russia's Bolshoi Opera gives its first performance outside the Soviet bloc, performing *Boris Godunov* at La Scala.

50-year-old mezz-soprano **Rise Stevens** has been named one of the general managers of the Metropolitan Opera's new national company.

BURYING THE HATCHET (BUT NOT IN EACH OTHER)

Metropolitan Opera manager **RUDOLF BING** and **MARIA MENEGHINI CALLAS** resolve their differences in Paris and the diva returns to the Met to star in *Tosca*.

Maria Callas

Leonard Bernstein takes a sabbatical for a year from the New York Philharmonic.

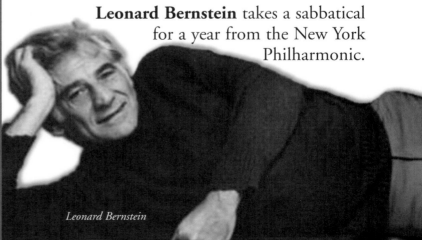

Leonard Bernstein

1964
DANCE
THE NEW YORK CITY BALLET

George Balanchine

Balanchine choreographs two new duets: *Meditation,* danced by **Suzanne Farrell** and **Jacques d'Amboise**, and *Tarantella*, danced by **Patricia McBride** and **Edward Villella**.

In celebration of the 400th anniversary of the birth of **William Shakespeare**, the New York City Ballet premieres *A Midsummer Night's Dream* to inaugurate the new State Theater at Lincoln Center, which is their new home.

With **Maria Tallchief, Patricia Wilde, Melissa Hayden, Arthur Mitchell** and **Andre Prokovsky** dancing, the New York City Ballet premieres *Quatuor*, a new ballet by **Jacques d'Amboise**.

A $5,000 grant to the New York City Ballet from the New York State Council on the Arts provides funding for small groups of dancers led by **Miss Hayden** and **Mr. Villella** to give free lecture-demonstrations in 30 New York City public schools.

Other Works Presented This Season

Clarinade
George Balanchine
Music: Morton Gould

Dim Lustre
Antony Tudor (written in 1943)
Music: Richard Strauss

Irish Fantasy
Jacques d'Amboise
Music: Charles Camille Saint-Saens

Piege de Lumière (American premiere)
John Taras
Music: Jean-Michel Damase

Swan Lake (one-act version)
George Balanchine (after Ivanov)
Music: Peter Ilyitch Tschaikovsky

Martha Graham

EN POINTE:

The Boston Ballet makes its debut as a professional company with appearances at the Boston Arts Festival presenting BALANCHINE'S *Donizetti Variations, Concerto Barocco* **and** *La Fille Mal Gardée.*

"An Evening with MARTHA GRAHAM" kicks off the Lincoln Center World's Fair Festival.

In a tribute to William Shakespeare, RUDOLPH NUREYEV and LYNN SEYMOUR of the Royal Ballet dance in ROBERT HELPMANN'S *Hamlet.*

In its second U.S. tour, Leningrad's Kirov Ballet presents *Raymonda,* **danced for the first time in America.**

The Ford Foundation gives a $155,000 grant to the Robert Joffrey Ballet.

Modern dance gets a lift when the New York State Council provides funds to the New York State Theater, making possible two performances by the American Dance Theater, directed by JOSÉ LIMÓN.

POPULAR DANCES
DONE TO ROCK 'N' ROLL MUSIC

Dog	Jerk	Hitchhiker
Monkey	Bug	Heat Wave
Pony	Swim	GoGo
Funky Chicken	Surf	Wobble
Bird	Popeye	Waddle
Fish	Frankenstein	Watusi
Hully Gully	High Life	Frug

HOT DISCOTHEQUES
Shepheard's (Manhattan)
Trudy Heller's (Manhattan)
Whisky a Go-Go (Los Angeles)

Discotheques become popular all over the world.

PASSING

Moe Gale, 65
Co-founder of Harlem's Savoy Ballroom, where the Lindy Hop, Count Basie and Ella Fitzgerald all got their start.

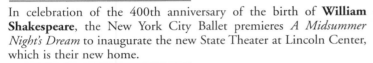

WHAT A YEAR IT WAS!

ON BROADWAY

TO DRINK OR NOT TO DRINK, THAT IS THE QUESTION

Elizabeth Taylor and Richard Burton have a champagne reception in his dressing room following Burton's performance in "Hamlet" at Toronto's O'Keefe Center.

600 celebrities gather to pay homage to Richard Burton and Elizabeth Taylor following Burton's opening in the Broadway production of "Hamlet."

Richard Burton

1964

ANOTHER OPENING, ANOTHER NIGHT

After The Fall

Any Wednesday

Baby Want A Kiss

The Ballad Of The Sad Café

Barefoot In The Park

Beekman Place

Ben Franklin In Paris

Blues For Mr. Charlie

But For Whom Charlie

Café Crown

Cambridge Circus

The Committee

The Deputy

Emlyn Williams *(left)* and **Jeremy Brett** *(right)* in *The Deputy*

1964

Josephine Baker

DYLAN

AN EVENING WITH
JOSEPHINE BAKER

FADE OUT ~
FADE IN

FIDDLER ON THE
ROOF

FOLIES BERGÈRE

FUNNY GIRL

GOLDEN BOY
☆
HELLO, DOLLY!
☆
HIGH SPIRITS
☆
INCIDENT AT VICHY
☆
THE KNACK
☆
LUV

ANOTHER
OPENING,
ANOTHER
NIGHT

Carol Channing in *Hello, Dolly!*

ANOTHER OPENING, ANOTHER NIGHT

OH WHAT A LOVELY WAR

✦

THE OWL AND THE PUSSYCAT

✦

THE PASSION OF JOSEF D

✦

THE PHYSICISTS

✦

THE SUBJECT WAS ROSES

✦

WHAT MAKES SAMMY RUN?

✦

THE WHITE HOUSE

OFF~ BROADWAY REVIVALS

The Maids
Jean Genet

•

The Zoo Story & The American Dream
Edward Albee

•

The Caretaker
Harold Pinter

•

The Immoralist
Andre Gide

FROM ACROSS THE SEA

THE COMEDY OF ERRORS
William Shakespeare

THE DYBBUK
S. Ansky

KING LEAR
William Shakespeare

LUTHER
John Osborne

CHIPS WITH EVERYTHING
Arnold Wesker

THE RESISTIBLE RISE OF ARTURO U
Bertolt Brecht

THE SEAGULL
Anton Chekhov

RIGHT YOU ARE IF YOU THINK YOU ARE
Luigi Pirandello

THE LOWER DEPTHS
Maxim Gorky

WHAT A YEAR IT WAS!

If you'd been making beautiful music till late last night,

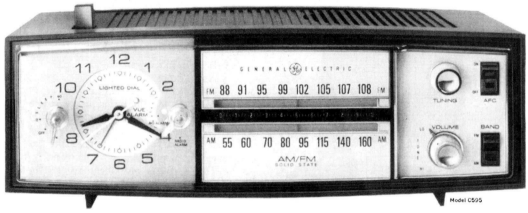

Model C595

would you look this good in the morning?
(The 1965 FM/AM Flair)

Neat, compact, long and low.

This handsome, new General Electric Flair brings out the best in any decor, from night-stand to knickknack shelf.

Brings out the best in sound, too.

Modern solid-state circuitry and a powerful four-inch Dynamic speaker play Bach on FM, the latest hits on AM. All with surprisingly rich tone and fidelity.

Extra features? Wakes you gently to sooth-ing music, for one thing. Or a buzzer. Or both.

Want an extra catnap? Tap that button on top. The G-E Snooz-Alarm® will shut off the alarm for your 40 winks—and turn it on again in about ten minutes.

Vue-Alarm lights up when alarm is set. Lighted-dial clock. Decoratively lighted dial panel. Walnut-grain finish on polystyrene.

All in all, this new General Electric Flair radio is the newest excitement in sound to-day. Isn't it about time you added some Flair to your life? Costs less than $70.*

*Actual price varies with dealer. Slightly higher West and South.

Radio Receiver Department, Utica, New York

GENERAL ⓖ ELECTRIC

97

THEY'LL CONTINUE SINGING FOR THEIR SUPPER

Actors in 18 Broadway shows return to work following the Actors' Equity settlement with the League of N.Y. Theaters calling for a $12.50 increase over a four-year period in their $117.50 weekly minimum pay.

● Designed to house the New York City Ballet and the Music Theater of Lincoln Center, the New York State Theater opens in April.

● Irish playwright **Brendan Behan** was out celebrating his release from the Royal City of Dublin Hospital but is back in Dublin's Meath Hospital with pneumonia and head injuries after he is found lying in a pool of blood.

● 34-year-old playwright **Lorraine Hansberry**, who is battling cancer, is in a coma at Manhattan's University Hospital.

● 63-year-old **Rudy Vallee** rounds off his third full year starring on Broadway in *How to Succeed in Business Without Really Trying*, staying with the show longer than any star in musical history.

In ceremonies at Stratford-upon-Avon, Prince Philip officially opens the 400th anniversary celebration of William Shakespeare's birth.

THE "I NEED TO GETS ME SOME MO' MONEY" BLUES

JAMES BALDWIN launches a last-minute fund-raising campaign to save his *"Blues for Mister Charlie,"* which is so in the red that it faces closure.

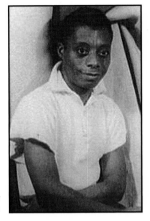

James Baldwin

Passings

Carol Haney, 39
Former chorus girl Haney won a Tony Award for her performance in *The Pajama Game*. She was the choreographer for *Flower Drum Song* and staged the musical numbers for *She Loves Me* and *Funny Girl*.

Cole Porter, 71
One of the great American songwriters, Yale grad Porter's many Broadway hit shows include *Can-Can, Kiss Me, Kate, Anything Goes, Gay Divorce, Silk Stockings* and *Jubilee*. Of the countless Porter songs, *Night and Day* and *I've Got You Under My Skin* (sung by many singers, in particular Frank Sinatra) are timeless American treasures.

Cole Porter

WHAT A YEAR IT WAS!

TONY AWARDS
1964

PLAY
LUTHER
John Osborne, playwright

•

MUSICAL PLAY
HELLO, DOLLY!

•

DRAMATIC ACTOR
Alec Guiness
DYLAN

•

DRAMATIC ACTRESS
Sandy Dennis
ANY WEDNESDAY

MUSICAL ACTOR
Bert Lahr
FOXY

•

MUSICAL ACTRESS
Carol Channing
HELLO, DOLLY!

NEW YORK DRAMA CRITICS' CIRCLE AWARDS

BEST PLAY	**LUTHER**
BEST MUSICAL	**HELLO, DOLLY!**
SPECIAL CITATION	**THE TROJAN WOMEN**

HELLO, DOLLY!
wins a record 10 awards.

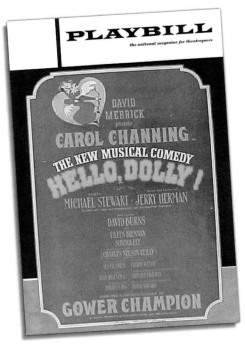

THE NATIONAL INSTITUTE OF
Arts and Letters
GOLD MEDAL AWARD

Lillian Hellman *Drama*
Ben Shahn *Graphic Art*

*No Pulitzer Prize for drama
is awarded this year.*

PRICE OF A
THEATER TICKET
$6.90

drop in the film...
the camera does the rest

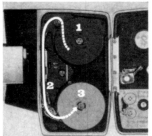

1 drop in the film
2 pull it to arrow
3 threads itself

New Yashica 8UL Power Zoom—
So Automatic It Threads Itself

The new Yashica 8UL movie camera is so automatic it even takes the worry out of film loading. Just drop in the spool and the camera threads itself perfectly, with no fumbling or fogging. You'll also like the electric operation, with two separate motors. One for the power zoom, the other to run the film. That way you can get exactly the scene you want before you shoot, without wasting film. The new CdS electric eye assures you of exactly the right exposure, even in dim light or with a single-beam movie light. You even focus through the crackling sharp Yashinon f/1.8 zoom lens, so you see exactly what you get on film. Other exciting features include manual and other special effects controls, remote control, viewfinder exposure signal, built-in filter and trigger pistol grip. Ask your dealer for a demonstration. Under **$190.**

Pistol grip extra.

SINGLE LENS REFLEXES
from $130. to $190.

TWIN-LENS REFLEXES
from $36. to $85.

35 mm's
from $55. to $100.

HALF FRAME
35 mm's—$45.

SUBMINIATURE $65.

for more information:

YASHICA®

YASHICA INC., 50-17 Queens Blvd.,
Woodside, N.Y. 11377 • Dept. 1

100

ART EVENTS IN THE BIG APPLE

33-year-old **Jasper Johns** has a career retrospective at the Jewish Museum.

In the first thorough exhibit of Nepali art, New York's Asia House presents paintings, manuscripts and sculpture from the small Himalayan kingdom.

Elaine de Kooning's premiere showing of her sculptures occurs at the "The Red Show" exhibition.

Jasper Johns

David Hockney is a new name in the New York art world and his work is shown at two local galleries.

New York artists come together to protest a plan to eliminate the Manhattan lofts where many of them work and live.

Andy Warhol's show at Stable Gallery features likenesses of favorite food and everyday items, including Kellogg's Corn Flakes, Brillo Soap Pads and Heinz's Ketchup. The wooden pieces can be had for $300-$600.

An **Edward Hopper** *retrospective of watercolors, oils, etchings and drawings is seen at the Whitney Museum, focusing on his work of the past two decades.*

"The American Supermarket," seen at Bianchini Gallery, is a smorgasbord of food items found in the typical American grocery store in this art-meets-performance art exhibit. **Andy Warhol** is on hand, autographing genuine Campbell's Soup cans, three for $18. **Claes Oldenburg** is represented by lifelike candy and pies, **Jasper Johns** by beer cans and **Roy Lichtenstein** by a turkey painting.

The Guggenheim Museum presents an **Alexander Calder** retrospective.

Celebrating what would have been **Toulouse-Lautrec's** 100th birthday, Wildenstein Gallery holds an exhibit featuring lithographs, posters, paintings and drawings.

Four galleries work together to present a retrospective of the work of **Georges Braque**—the first exhibit of his work in America in 15 years.

An Edward Hopper etching

WHAT A YEAR IT WAS!

1964

NEW YORK WORLD'S FAIR

The Spanish Pavilion features several paintings by **Goya**, as well as works by **Dali** and **El Greco**.

A fifth-century statue of Buddha adorns the Indian Pavilion.

Dotting the landscape around Kennedy Plaza are enormous sculptures by **Louise Nevelson, Isamu Noguchi, Reuben Nakian** and **Alexander Calder**.

Rome's St. Peters loans **Michelangelo's** "Pieta" to the Vatican Pavilion.

OH SAY CAN YOU SEE. . .

The Smithsonian Institution's Museum of History and Technology opens. One of the prized pieces is the actual flag that was the inspiration for *The Star-Spangled Banner*.

Maine's Colby College presents a show entitled "Maine—100 Artists of the 20th Century," which includes pieces by **John Marin, Georgia O'Keeffe, Edward Hopper** and **Andrew Wyeth**.

Jackson Pollock's "Convergence" is reproduced as a puzzle.

This year's "Carnegie International" is a no-holds-barred look at mostly modern works with **George Segal's** life-size sculpture "The Bus Riders" seen alongside **Picasso, Bacon** and **Giacometti** paintings, **de Kooning's** "Woman V," **Oldenburg's** "Boxers in Box" and **Jim Dine's** "Three Palettes (Portrait of A)." **Ellsworth Kelly's** "Blue, Black and Red" wins the $2,000 prize.

Segal's Bus Riders

Ground is broken in Los Angeles for a Hollywood Museum.

One of the great art events of the year, a comprehensive **Pierre Bonnard** exhibit is mounted jointly by the Los Angeles County Art Museum, the Museum of Modern Art and the Art Institute of Chicago.

Lithograph by Bonnard

WHAT A YEAR IT WAS!

The Guggenheim Museum auctions off 50 works by Vasily Kandinsky.

FOUR SCORE AND $3.00

A perceptive shopper in a thrift shop spots a small oil painting and pays $3.00 for what turns out to be the earliest known picture of President Abraham Lincoln.

London-based Sotheby's acquires 75% of New York's Parke-Bernet.

AT LEAST IT HAS PICTURES ON BOTH SIDES

The Metropolitan Museum purchases a two-sided **Raphael** drawing for $89,600, the most ever paid for a drawing. One side features the baby Jesus, the Virgin Mary and St. John the Baptist while a nude appears on the other side.

A **Peter Paul Rubens** canvas worth $200,000 is stolen from the Brussels Museum of Ancient Art, but luckily is recovered several days later.

POP GOES THE ART WORLD – NEW PIECES

Roy Lichtenstein	*Crying Girl*	**Jasper Johns**	*Field Painting*
Roy Lichtenstein	*As I Opened Fire*	**Louise Nevelson**	*Black Cord*
Jim Dine	*Palette (Self-Portrait No. 1)*	**Andy Warhol**	*Jackie, 1964*
Edward Kienholz	*Back Seat Dodge*		
Edward Kienholz	*The Birthday*		
Robert Rauschenberg	*Retroactive 1*		
Jasper Johns	*Ale Cans*		

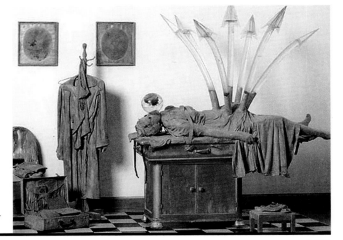

Kienholz's The Birthday

32nd VENICE BIENNALE TIDBITS

Robert Rauschenberg wins the Grand Prize for Painting, the first time an American has ever won the coveted award.

Because of some nude works, the Roman Catholic Patriarch of Venice forbids priests and nuns to attend the Biennale.

34 countries, 500 artists and 3,000 paintings are included in the show.

Departing from previous tradition, American artists represent America and not individual sponsors. Among the many artists participating on behalf of the United States are **Johns, Oldenburg, Rauschenberg, Dine** and **Stella**.

The Louvre allows *Whistler's Mother* to travel to several U.S. museums. It also loans *Venus de Milo* to the Tokyo Museum of Western Art. The priceless marble statue is slightly damaged in transit.

Celebrating the 400th anniversary of his death, 1964 is the year of **Michelangelo** in Rome. A wooden crucifix, discovered only last year, is unveiled to the public.

Robert Rauschenberg creates designs in Venice, Italy for Merce Cunningham's ballet troupe.

"Picasso and Man," a retrospective of the master's works from the turn-of-the-century through the present day, is jointly mounted by the Museum of Fine Arts in Montreal and the Art Gallery of Toronto.

Billy Rose visits Jerusalem to keep an eye on construction of a garden that will permanently exhibit $1 million worth of his sculptures.

PASSINGS

Stuart Davis, 69
American abstract painter who used bright colors and everyday themes in his work. He received two Guggenheim International Awards and a Guggenheim Fellowship.

Anson Conger Goodyear, 86
President of the Museum of Modern Art from 1929–39, Goodyear put together a show of Gauguin, Van Gogh, Seurat and Cezanne, presenting the painters to the U.S. for the first time.

Rico Lebrun, 63
Expressionist painter, illustrator, college art teacher and stained glass designer, Lebrun helped create the image of Bambi at Disney Studios.

Rico Lebrun's
Crucifixion

WHAT A YEAR IT WAS!

Books

Nobel Prize for Literature

JEAN-PAUL SARTRE, France

"For his work which, rich in ideas and filled with the spirit of freedom and the quest for truth, has exerted a far-reaching influence on our age."

The award is declined by Sartre.

Pulitzer Prizes

HISTORY
Puritan Village: The Formation Of A New England Town   SUMNER CHILTON POWELL

BIOGRAPHY OR AUTOBIOGRAPHY
John Keats   WALTER JACKSON BATE

POETRY
At The End Of The Open Road   LOUIS SIMPSON

GENERAL NON-FICTION
Anti-Intellectualism In American Life   RICHARD HOFSTADTER

American Academy of Arts & Letters

AWARD OF MERIT
JOHN O'HARA

Caldecott Award
(Children's Picture Book)

Where The Wild Things Are
MAURICE SENDAK

National Book Award
(Fiction)

The Centaur, JOHN UPDIKE

Truman Capote, James Baldwin, Ralph Ellison and John Updike are among the new authors elected to the National Institute of Arts & Letters.

$10 million is raised for the John F. Kennedy Memorial Library at Harvard University. A touring exhibit of Kennedy's personal effects helps raise money for the project.

Novelists John Cheever and John Updike visit the Soviet Union and share vodka with Russian poet **Evgeny Evtushenko**.

The Soviet Communist Party's Ideological Commission condemns an anti-Semitic book that depicts Jewish people negatively. Tass also censures the paperback, as do foreign organizations.

The U.S. Supreme Court rules against the Florida Supreme Court's ban on **Henry Miller's** *Tropic of Cancer.* The Illinois Supreme Court, however, rules against the book, declaring it obscene.

PAPERBACK WRITER

300 million paperback books are published in the U.S.

POCKET BOOKS **celebrates its 25th anniversary.**

COOKING, CLEANING—WHAT'S NOT TO LOVE?

Sort of the anti-Betty Friedan, Phyllis McGinley's *Sixpence in Her Shoe* **espouses the life of a housewife.**

Books

A Little Learning
Evelyn Waugh

A Mother's Kisses
Bruce Jay Friedman

A Moveable Feast
Ernest Hemingway
(posthumously)

A Very Easy Death
Simone de Beauvoir

The Act Of Creation
Arthur Koestler

Armageddon
Leon Uris

Around About America
Erskine Caldwell

The Brigadier And The Golf Widow
John Cheever

Children Of Violence: Martha Quest And A Proper Marriage
Doris Lessing

Chitty Chitty Bang Bang
Ian Fleming

Come Back, Dr. Caligari
Donald Barthelme

The Complete Poems Of D.H. Lawrence

Dallas Justice: The Real Story Of Jack Ruby and His Trial
Melvin Belli

The Far Field
Theodore Roethke
(posthumously)

Flood: A Romance Of Our Time
Robert Penn Warren

God And Golem, Inc.
Norbert Wiener

Herzog
Saul Bellow

How It Is
Samuel Beckett

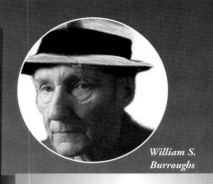

William S. Burroughs

I Need All The Friends I Can Get
Charles M. Schulz

If Morning Ever Comes
Anne Tyler

If You Take Baloney And Cut It Yup You Get Baloney: This Is Gestalt Spelled Backwards
William S. Burroughs

In His Own Write
John Lennon

The Italian Girl
Iris Murdoch

Julian
Gore Vidal

The Keepers Of The House
Shirley Ann Grau

Ernest Hemingway

Last Exit To Brooklyn
Hubert Selby Jr.

•

Life With Picasso
Françoise Gilot

•

Little Big Man
Thomas Berger

•

The Little Girls
Elizabeth Bowen

•

The Man
Irving Wallace

•

My Autobiography
Charles Chaplin

•

Nothing Personal
Richard Avedon &
James Baldwin

•

Nova Express
William S. Burroughs

**The Official
Warren
Commission
Report On
The Assassination
Of President
John F. Kennedy**

•

**One Day In The
Afternoon Of
The World**
William Saroyan

•

**One Fat
Englishman**
Kingsley Amis

•

**Point Of
The Lance**
Sargent Shriver

•

**The Rector
Of Justin**
Louis Auchincloss

•

Reminiscences
General Douglas
MacArthur

•

Reporting
Lillian Ross

Reuben, Reuben
Peter De Vries

•

The Scarperer
Brendan Behan

•

Second Skin
John Hawkes

•

**Selected Letters
Of Robert Frost**

•

Short Friday
Isaac Bashevis Singer

•

**The Wapshot
Scandal**
John Cheever

•

**With Shuddering
Fall**
Joyce Carol Oates

•

Why We Can't Wait
Dr. Martin Luther King Jr.

•

The Words
Jean-Paul Sartre

•

You Only Live Twice
Ian Fleming

Robert Frost

Two roads diverged in a wood, and I—
I took the one less traveled by,
And that has made all the difference.

Robert Frost's daughter bequeaths her father's 3,000 books to New York University, and not Amherst College as expected.

Ian Fleming sells 51% of his James Bond royalties, netting $280,000.

For $2,750,000, Chicago's Newberry Library purchases a privately owned rare book and manuscript collection which includes first editions of **Shakespeare**, **Aristotle** and **Homer**, *Alice in Wonderland, The Faerie Queene, Don Quixote* and *Uncle Tom's Cabin.*

NOW THAT'S EDUCATION!
To help celebrate National Education Day, hundreds of foreign-written textbooks are burned in Jakarta, Indonesia.

The New Republic turns 50.

Henry Luce resigns as editor-in-chief of Time Inc.

FAMOUS BIRTH | **Bret Easton Ellis**

PASSINGS

Ian Fleming, 56
Creator of British agent James Bond, whose worldwide adventures are chronicled in a multitude of books, including *Live and Let Die, Diamonds Are Forever, From Russia with Love, Dr. No* and *Goldfinger.* He also wrote *Chitty Chitty Bang Bang* for his son.

Grace Metalious, 39
Author of *Peyton Place.* With over 300,000 hardback and 8 million paperbacks sold, it is the most successful novel in American history.

Flannery O'Connor, 39
Short story writer and novelist, whose tales often depict Southern life in a morbid manner, O'Connor received many O'Henry awards and a Ford Foundation grant.

Roy Wilson Howard, 81
A former reporter, Howard was president of the United Press, and eventually chairman of the board and president of Scripps-Howard newspapers.

FASHION 1964

"WINNIE" WINNER
COTY
AMERICAN FASHION CRITICS AWARD
GEOFFREY BEENE **JACQUES TIFFEAU**

IT'S A MOD, MOD, MOD, MOD WORLD

The British Mod style, made popular by Mary Quant and other young designers, becomes vogue in America. The world's favorite British band, the Beatles, also influence fashion choices made by the young and hip set.

MOD FASHION
icons such as BARBRA STREISAND join perennially well-dressed mavens like the DUCHESS OF WINDSOR and JACKIE KENNEDY.

The biggest splash of the year is **RUDI GERNREICH's** topless bathing suit. It makes headlines around the world and a young model is arrested in Chicago for wearing it.

Lots of décolletage is shown, both night and day, partially influenced by the film TOM JONES.

Betsey Johnson
wins the Guest Editor Contest for **Mademoiselle**.

President Johnson's Texas roots spread all over Washington, D.C. as he gives away dozens of cowboy hats to friends and colleagues.

18-year-old model **CANDICE BERGEN** poses for the covers of **GLAMOUR**, **LADIES' HOME JOURNAL** and **MADEMOISELLE**.

WHAT A YEAR IT WAS!

1964

GERMAN PREPARE BY MARDI

Exotic feathers with a definite carnival mood.

WHAT A YEAR IT WAS!

STYLISTS
FOR SPRING
UNVEILING THEIR
GRAS HATS

1964

Here's a perky pirate.

Our hats are off to the designers on this enchanting number.

There's fruit for eating and ah well, this fruit is made for wearing.

A PRODUCT OF *Ford* MOTOR COMPANY · LINCOLN-MERCURY DIVISION

MERCURY, CHOSEN BY SQUAW VALLEY LODGE, TAHOE CITY, CALIF., (SHOWN HERE) AS THEIR COURTESY CAR FOR SPECIAL GUESTS

Try to act nonchalant driving the 1965 Mercury. | Just try. | It's now in the Lincoln Continental tradition.

What's changed? Just about everything. You can see the changes in the graceful new proportions, in the long, low thrusting hood. You can feel the changes in the ride—the solid, smooth, superbly quiet ride. For this Mercury is built in the Lincoln Continental tradition. See the difference at your Mercury dealer's. Discover why Mercury is now the official courtesy car at Squaw Valley.

 Mercury

now in the Lincoln Continental tradition

134 million pairs of sunglasses are sold in America.

IS THE GLASS HALF EMPTY?

Half-specs, such as those worn by Benjamin Franklin, are the trendy glasses for nearsighted folks.

Sandals **are the shoe of choice and are worn by squares and hipsters alike. Some are simple, some are bejeweled, some are inexpensive and some cost well over $100.**

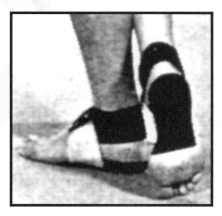

Stretch fabrics,

made with spandex, are the hottest new thing in comfort, and show up in all sorts of sportswear including skirts, jumpsuits, shirts and denim.

Stockings

Lounging pajamas

for entertaining at home are all the rage. **t**hey are wide-legged, hip-hugging, multihued and might even show a bit of the tummy or back. Silk jumpsuits are another option for the woman willing to take a chance with pants.

... are colorful, textured, have different patterns and help a gal stay warm under short skirts.

Italian designer **EMILIO PUCCI** looks to the east for influences, and comes up with harem pants and dresses, saris, tunics and many colorful pieces.

MAINBOCHER uses lots of white in his spring collection.

WHAT A YEAR IT WAS!

1964 PARI

AT COURRÈGES...

He surprises the fashion world by moving hemlines above the knee. At the other extreme, he designs blouses that conceal everything apart from the hands and face. Courrèges also begins showing slacks for outside the home. Mod pink boots, hip-hugging pants, bonnets that tie under the chin and double-breasted suits are all shown on Courrèges' runway.

AT CHANEL...

Always a trendsetter, the first lady of fashion designs pants with wide legs, some with a sailor look. It's her first pants collection in decades. Her classic tweed suits have a bit of lamé and silk mixed in, either in the suit or the accompanying blouse. Mme. Chanel goes for texture with a white linen suit, and uses lots of pastel colors.

AT DIOR...

Marc Bohan's style continues to attract legions of fans all around the world. The variety at the House of Dior in 1964 includes crepe blouses over long skirts, organdie pajamas for home, large prints and patterns, straw hats, tweeds, velvets, turtlenecks, double-breasted jackets, berets and slim shapes.

116

S KARL LAGERFELD
begins designing for Chloe.

1964

SAINT LAURENT...

The young designer shows wool suits, silk blouses, slender sleeves, gloves, tunic skirts and taffeta bows on hats. He introduces his first perfume, Y.

AT GIVENCHY...

Audrey Hepburn's good friend and favorite designer, Hubert de Givenchy, offers vivid hues, turbans and princess silhouettes for the classic stylish woman.

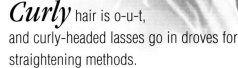

WHAT'S "IN" FOR YOUR FACE & HAIR

blondes do have more fun, this year anyway, as light-colored hair is in, in, in.

hairsprays with sunscreen are now available.

Hair bows are made popular by Chanel, and seen everywhere.

Long bangs are in with the Mod crowd.

Curly hair is o-u-t, and curly-headed lasses go in droves for straightening methods.

ouches

the eyes are best defined by light eyebrows and kangaroo eyes with lashes curled down.

Revlon's newest luscious lip colors include Passionata Pink, Caramella and Coralissimo.

Some lipsticks have traces of pearl and gold.

Lipsticks that taste like cherry, peppermint and other flavors enter the marketplace.

Decidedly Neat

Dress shirts made casual by the checks, stripes and plaids.

FOR HIM
FOR HIM
and Casual

Rain or shine, the polyester and cotton keeps its crisp looks.

A stretch in the slacks are easy on the strides.

PASSINGS

JULIEN ARPELS, 79

Van Cleef & Arpels jewelers opened for business in Paris in 1906, headed by three Arpels brothers— Julien, Charles and Louis—and their brother-in-law, Alfred Van Cleef. At the time of his death, Julien was president of the company.

FRED COLE, 63

Bathing suit designer and founder of the Cole of California swimwear line.

Launched on August 19, 1964

Syncom III is "parked" 22,300 miles
above the Pacific, at the International Date Line

WHERE TODAY MEETS TOMORROW

This NASA/Hughes communications
satellite connects the Far East and West with
24-hour uninterrupted TV and radio.

From its vantage point over the Pacific, the historic Syncom III can "see" a third of the earth. It brings to practical reality a dream of ages — giving mankind uninterrupted trans-Pacific communications.

One of its first achievements will be to bring the 1964 Tokyo Olympic Games "live" into your living room. But it will also open a new era in improved telephone and other types of communications.

Built for NASA by Hughes, this satellite is another step forward in the development of a satellite communications system which will be affordable for all the nations of the earth.

An earlier Syncom has been operating successfully for more than a year. *Next* year, a Hughes Syncom-type satellite will be put over the Atlantic for the Communications Satellite Corporation. "Public Satellite #1" — it will bring Europe close as your phone and TV set.

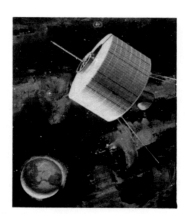

| HUGHES |

HUGHES AIRCRAFT COMPANY

Products like Syncom, devised to let
mankind share in the fruits of science, illustrate how
Hughes is creating a new world with electronics.

New PRODUCTS & INVENTIONS

1964

HERE'S LOOKING AT YOU

Bell introduces the *Picturephone* with a conversation between Lady Bird Johnson in Washington, D.C. and Dr. Elizabeth A. Wood at the New York labs.

A HOME TELEVISION RECORDER IS DEMONSTRATED IN NEW YORK.

LOOK OUT, MUSICIANS' UNION

Robert A. Moog engineers the first commercial music synthesizer.

BILL BANE of La Canada, California is *Science Digest's* **Inventor of the Month** with the development of his "Bane Patch" to help heal a horse's cracked hoof.

FORD INTRODUCES THE SPORTY new MUSTANG

to attract the new youth market and sells a record one million cars in the first 12 months.

POP-TARTS
make their way into children's tummies for the first time.

They've Taken To Drink

Presidential candidate Barry Goldwater produces a soft drink called Goldwater, distributed by the Gold-Water Distributing Company out of Granite City, Illinois. Not to be outdone, opponent Lyndon Johnson counters with Johnson Juice, distributed by the Ladybird Distributing Company, also located in Granite City, Illinois.

JUST BOIL THE WATER AND POUR

MAXIM, the first freeze-dried coffee, is developed by General Foods.

Pepsi-Cola introduces sugar-free Diet Pepsi.

ATTENTION, TURKEY CARVERS
General Electric is marketing a new electric knife for $27.95.

EASY LIFTOFF

Coca-Cola introduces the industry's first lift-top cans and bottles with lift-top crowns.

self opening
pop top
beer cap

Pop-Up

WHAT A YEAR IT WAS!

YOUR VERY OWN DRAFT BEER IN YOUR FRIDGE

National Can Company of Chicago is manufacturing the new one-gallon disposable "Tap-A-Keg" can for home use that keeps beer fresh for up to four weeks.

TICK TOCK

A transistorized metronome is being offered for the first time.

RCA is offering a swivel-base color television that allows the set to be turned to face anywhere in the room.

A WORKING CHAIR LADY

Available in a wide choice of designer fabrics, the **CASTRO READY LADY CHAIR** is an easy-chair that comes equipped with an attached folding ironing board, a steam iron, a hair dryer and cord and plug connection for electrical outlets.

FOR ALL YOU ASHES OUT THERE

For those of you who like to smoke in the dark, Glo-Lite Products is offering a luminous ashtray that glows in the dark.

INSTANT ANTIQUES

A new do-it-yourself kit for creating an antique look on furniture is being offered by **Martin-Senour Co**. of Chicago, Illinois.

New Sears refrigerator has automatic ice-maker—ends emptying and filling trays

Amazing automatic ice-maker gives you an endless supply of ice, separated into tidy pieces and ready to drop into your glass. See it in the Coldspot refrigerator. Now <u>on sale</u> at Sears, Roebuck and Co.

WHY go through life tussling with ice-cube trays when this sleek new Coldspot has a container of ice waiting for you whenever you need it?

MODEL NO. W16E1M (CATALOG NO. W4652)

SAVE $60 DURING JUNE ONLY

All you pay for this new 16.5 cu. ft. refrigerator is $349.00* (regularly $409.95). Zip into your Sears store or catalog sales office for a look. The colors are pink, yellow, turquoise, white, and shaded coppertone.

Just reach in. Scoop out all you need. And the Coldspot's busy little ice-maker will make up a fresh supply *fast*. You don't even have to fill it with water!

The ice-maker not only *makes* ice automatically—it also empties the ice into the storage container automatically. And then *shuts off* by itself.

The container holds up to 180 pieces of ice. Yet the ice-maker is so compact that it occupies no more shelf space than a regular set of ice-cube trays. See for yourself—in the upper left-hand corner of the refrigerator shown here.

Up to 12 percent <u>more</u> food space

Sears recently lined up three brand-new refrigerators, all famous makes you've seen advertised in magazines. Each was the equivalent, in measured volume, of the Coldspot on the left. Yet the Coldspot held more food than *any* of its competitors (in one case, a full 12 percent more).

One secret of all that extra space is the ingenious way the Coldspot's Spacemaster shelves and crispers adjust. The picture shows one of literally *hundreds* of different ways you can arrange these shelves.

Even the door shelves are adjustable. Notice how each one can be arranged on *two* levels. You'd be surprised how much extra food you can fit in this way. All in all, a 16.5 cubic foot Coldspot—with its Spacemaster shelving—does the work of an ordinary 18 cubic foot refrigerator.

Forget defrosting problems

Coldspot engineers have also come up with a new way to keep frost from forming—even inside the extra-large freezer. Hence, no defrosting. Ever. And remember—you pay no money down on Sears credit plans.

Satisfaction guaranteed or your money back.

*Price includes normal delivery, and is slightly higher in Alaska, Hawaii, and Puerto Rico. Small extra charge for connecting ice-maker.

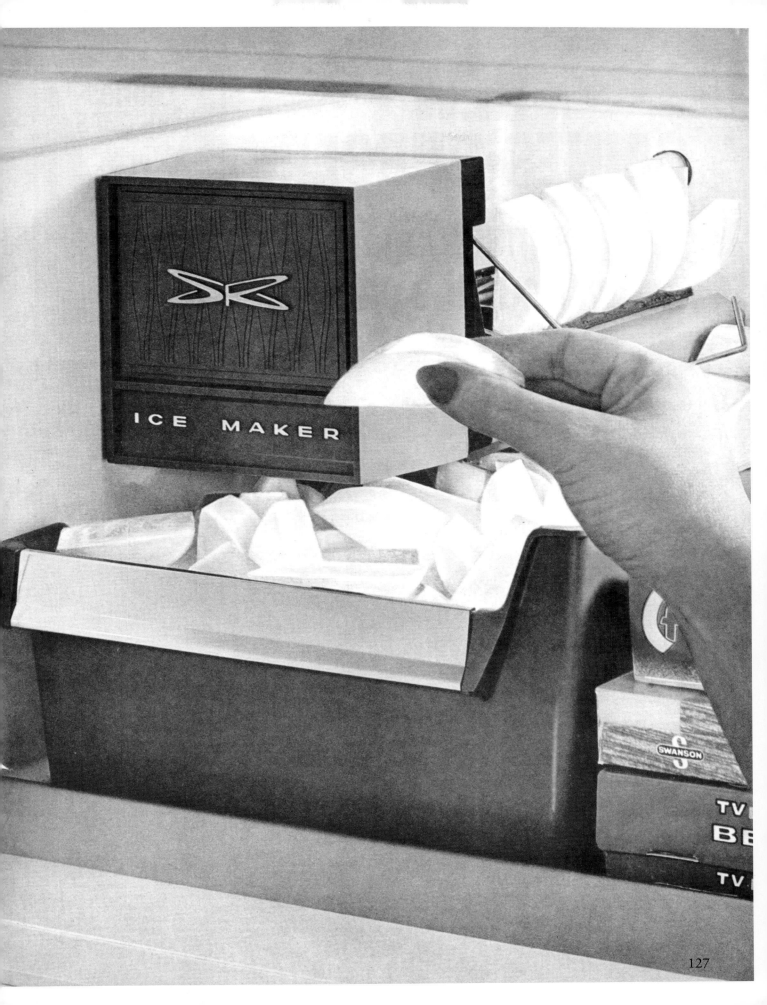

1964

SNOOPING ON THE STREET WHERE YOU LIVE

A new mobile electronic gadget enables pollsters to determine from the street if your television set is turned on and to what channel it is tuned.

Burroughs Corp. launches its new *Direct Accounting Computer*, which can generate sales, inventory and other business reports.

The Bendix Corp. introduces the *Watercom*, a new underwater communications system that enables a diver to talk to others beneath the surface of the water within a range of 100 yards.

An Oakland, California company develops the *Call Diverter*, which electronically switches incoming calls from one telephone to another regardless of the location.

A STRIKING NEW LOOK

A new top-opening paper self-closing matchbook, which doesn't have to be closed before striking, has been developed by **Click Bookmatch Inc.** of Ownings Mills, Maryland. The new cover has 25% more space for advertising inside, which is good news for the $30 million matchbook advertising industry.

A professor of psychology at Rutgers University in New Jersey, in conjunction with engineers from the Thomas A. Edison Research Laboratory, has developed a talking typewriter as a teaching aid for children.

AT&T introduces a revolutionary device for conducting business—**Telpak**, a wideband, bulk communications service permitting flexible use by big customers of computer-based facsimile and other types of data.

THE BETTER TO SEE YOU WITH

For cutting out the glare in nighttime driving, you can now buy antiglare glasses with plastic amber lenses.

LEAVING YOU IN THE DARK

Corning develops photochromic lenses that darken in the sun.

IS IT BEATING OR ISN'T IT?

A new device called the **Cardio-Sensor** can detect heart activity that a stethoscope can't, thus allowing a physician to determine whether or not a patient is still alive.

AN INSTANT BIG CHILL

Medi-Cold is an emergency, reusable ice pack that is activated by shaking the bag and snapping the ends.

During the Firecracker 400 at Daytona Beach, Florida, race driver Bobby Isaac tests a special garment designed to keep APOLLO astronauts cool during their space travels.

COULD KNOCK THE BITE RIGHT OUT OF THEM

British postmen might soon be equipped with a small aerosol container filled with a mild eye irritant to squirt at an attacking dog.

GETTING A "FIN" UP

Plans have been drawn up for fish "ladders" between Oregon and Washington that will water-lift salmon, enabling them to continue their normal migrations and trips upstream to spawning areas by passing over dams.

SNAKE OIL THAT REALLY WORKS

James R. Jenni of Oklahoma City, Oklahoma wins a patent for a poison that kills cold-blooded creatures. In a test in a snake-infested area of Texas, 248 snakes die three days after the area is sprayed with the toxicant.

AUTOMOBILE • AUTOMOBILE

CADILLAC introduces Climate Control, a fully automatic air-conditioning system.

THE DRIVOMETER, a new mechanism that fits in the glove compartment, is designed to test a driver's skill on the road and is expected to be useful in road tests, driver instruction and traffic engineering.

B.F. GOODRICH COMPANY patents a tire that folds and can be stored in the glove compartment.

Could Discourage Nose Picking

A two-camera closed-circuit television system designed to monitor traffic conditions is being used in Northern California.

PASSINGS

LEOPOLD MANNES, 64
Co-creator of Kodachrome film.

ATAULLAH OZAI-DURRANI, 66
Inventor of Minute Rice.

CHARLES FRANKLIN SEABROOK, 83
Co-creator of frozen foods. The fresh vegetables for Birds Eye foods came from Seabrook's farm.

RUSSELL GAMES SLAYTER, 67
Creator of Fiberglas.

HENRY WALDEN, 80
Inventor of the moving electric news sign in Times Square, Walden also made and flew the first monoplane in America.

WHAT A YEAR IT WAS!

THE ROYAL TOUCH

In portable typewriters for students, it means the easiest handling, fastest operating, liveliest typing, dreamiest looking portables for back-to-school.

Press. And zing! You've set a margin. Push. And zip! You've set a column for figures or words. Snap. And click! You've changed a ribbon with a smudgeproof cartridge. These are the rapid sounds, the conveniences of the automatic features on the Royal Safari® portable. Features that make schoolwork go faster, easier, livelier. They're all part of the Royal engineering ingenuity—The Royal Touch—you'll find in *every* Royal portable. Precision portables. Dependable portables. Rugged portables with a 5-year guarantee*. The portables to go back to school with and type up a storm of better grades.

*Royal McBee guarantees replacement at no charge, other than labor and shipping, of any defective part (except rubber parts, ribbons, or parts damaged by accident or misuse) within 5 years of purchase. No labor charge within first 90 days. Guarantee covers only the original purchaser.

ROYAL® McBEE
CORPORATION

The Royal Safari, the portable with all the automatic features of the Royal office typewriter. Royal portables start at $49.95, with case.

Every year more Royal typewriters are bought in America than any other brand.

SCIENCE & medicine

AMERICAN HEART ASSOCIATION'S
1964 RESEARCH AWARD

Dr. Rebecca C. Lancefield
Rockefeller Institute
(First woman recipient of this prize)

Dr. Muriel Roger of the Rockefeller Institute reports that she has successfully transplanted a single gene with the receiving cell subsequently displaying the specific hereditary trait.

A new test for detecting and locating many hidden cancers has been developed by **Dr. Myron Arlen** of New York's Memorial Hospital.

NATION'S OLDEST LIVING DOCTOR
Katheryn Haage Swartz, 103

The Supreme Court leaves standing a decision by a lower court that any hospital built with federal aid may not segregate its patients or its staff.

SATELLITE SYNCOM III

transmits live the Summer Olympic games across the Pacific from Japan.

The first **U.S. Gemini** test flight orbits earth three times.

OMEGA-MINUS, a new subatomic particle, is discovered by a group of physicists at the Brookhaven National Laboratory in New York.

Great Britain struggles with a "brain drain" as many of their scientists emigrate to the U.S.

RETIREMENT LIFE EXPECTANCY:
6.5 YEARS

EXTRA
SPACE

1964

HELICOPTERS BECOME IMPORTANT WEAPONS

U.S. Army helicopter pilots in Germany prepare to try out new techniques while testing an improved M-6 machine gun.

They have developed skills that enable them to zoom, dart and dodge across the countryside.

The new M-6 machine gun should make it safer for the foot soldier to do his job.

When the pilot spots an enemy outpost, he can drop down behind hedges to dodge enemy fire until it's safe to resume altitude. Army authorities feel that this new hedge-hopping capability will enable them to move the foot soldier with greater speed.

The helicopter has come a long way in a few short years, and now flying techniques take a big step ahead.

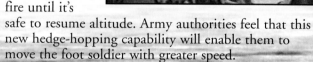

132

AN EXPLOSIVE SUBJECT

UP IN SMOKE

China detonates its first atomic bomb, sending shock waves around the world.

Over 3,500 scientists and industrial observers from around the world gather in Geneva to attend the U.N.'s Third International Conference on Peaceful Uses of Atomic Energy.

IT IS EXPECTED THAT FRANCE WILL BE ENDING ITS NUCLEAR TESTING PROGRAM IN THE ALGERIAN SAHARA.

atomic

The U.S. Atomic Energy Commission agrees to sell 770 pounds of plutonium for $3-1/2 million to the European Atomic Energy Community.

A White House task force reports that huge nuclear power plants could be built by 1975 to supply cheap electricity and simultaneously produce large amounts of fresh water from the oceans.

GOOD NEWS IF YOU'RE A RAT

Reporting on the results of a six-year study of the effects of radiation on mice, a UCLA professor concludes that radiation may not be as dangerous as we think and that in a nuclear world, man may survive without turning into mutations.

THE SCIENTIFIC COMMITTEE ON RADIATION REPORTS A 33% DECREASE IN NUCLEAR FALLOUT WORLDWIDE, WHICH THEY ATTRIBUTE TO THE NUCLEAR TEST BAN.

1964

It's all in the stars, dear

NASA tests first successful rocket engine.

Americans watch on television as the **Saturn 1** rocket is put into orbit with a 10-ton payload, the heaviest in history, enabling the U.S. to surpass the Soviet Union for the first time.

The U.S. sends up the passive communications satellite **Echo 2**, a 135-foot plastic and aluminum-foil balloon designed to reflect radio signals from one point on the earth to another. The Soviets pick up a signal near Gorki, making the transmission the first joint U.S.-British-Soviet venture.

Is that Swiss or Cheddar?

Equipped with six television cameras, **Ranger 7** transmits 4,316 close-up photos of the moon before crashing into the surface of the moon, revealing portions of the moon's surface as being suitable for manned landings and that it is not covered with a deep layer of dust.

President Johnson discloses that the U.S. has developed in secrecy a jet plane, the A-11, capable of sustained flight at more than 2,000 mph and at altitudes of more than 70,000 feet.

Explorers

Two scientific U.S. satellites—**Explorers 24 and 25**—are launched into near-polar orbit from Vandenberg Air Force Base.

Explorer 26, designed to provide data on how high-energy particles are injected, trapped and eventually lost in the Van Allen radiation belts, is launched from Cape Kennedy.

Soviets

Manned with three people, the Soviet spacecraft *Voskhod 1*, the first to carry more than one person, makes 16 orbits before returning safely to earth.

The Soviet Union sets a new distance record for radar by bouncing signals 370 million miles to Jupiter and back.

The U.S. sends up **Mariner 4**, an unmanned interplanetary probe launched toward Mars.

The U.S. carries out 70 unmanned orbital and deep-space flights this year, compared with about 40 conducted by the Soviets.

A satellite to monitor solar X-rays is launched by the Navy from the Pacific Missile Range at California's Vandenberg Air Force Base.

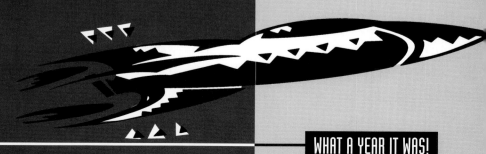

Brutus

Star Light, Star Bright

Radio star 3C-147, estimated at several billion light-years away and the most distant celestial object discovered to date, is identified by two California astronomers through photographs from the Mt. Wilson and Palomar Observatories.

Using a laser beam, researchers from Bell Telephone Laboratories in New Jersey determine that some craters on the moon are 20,000 feet deep.

A "PHYSIZZLING" OF PHYSICISTS IS PREDICTED

The American Institute of Physicists warns that if current trends continue, there will be only 38,000 physicists to fill 59,300 jobs by 1970.

RCA Communications

demonstrates the world's first computerized telegraph system.

Bell Telephone Laboratories

breaks new ground with computers with their 17-minute animated cartoon made by using a computer linked to a cathode-ray tube and a movie camera.

LOOK magazine pioneers the first three-dimensional photograph ever to be printed in the millions.

IN THE DRINK

The world's first nuclear-powered lighthouse opens on Maryland's Chesapeake Bay.

The International Hydrological Decade is created in an attempt to solve some of the world's water problems.

COUGH, COUGH, SPUTTER, SPUTTER

In an effort to clean up its smog problem, California's Motor Vehicle Pollution Control Board approves a device for use on all 1966 cars which will help eliminate unburned hydrocarbons from auto exhausts.

No house calls today!

Calling the new law a step toward socialized medicine, 10,000 Belgian doctors close their offices and leave their hospitals to go on strike.

Hoping to make their hospital stay a bit more cheerful, patients at San Francisco's Mount Zion Hospital are being offered a glass of sherry, port or burgundy with their dinner.

SOMETHING TO BARK ABOUT

Using optical glass fibers, which are passed through a dog's aortic valve opening and closing, heart specialist Walter Gamble reports the first known film taken from inside the organ.

Not just a lot of hot air

Following his examination of 40 professional wind instrumentalists, a doctor at Emory University School of Medicine suggests that playing a wind instrument such as clarinet or flute could be ideal for chronic asthmatics as it causes inflation of lungs to near capacity and deep exhalation while playing.

HEART-LUNG MACHINES substitute sugar-water solutions for blood, allowing surgeons to proceed without a large number of donors.

A Collective Snore

Viral encephalitis, also known as sleeping sickness, hits Houston in epidemic proportions with 700 cases, including 32 deaths, reported by October 1st.

HOME DIALYSIS IS INTRODUCED FOR KIDNEY PATIENTS.

You Gotta Have Heart

DR. SEYMOUR RINZLER reports to the American Public Health Association that middle-aged men who replace the animal fats and dairy products in their diets with vegetable oils and fish suffer a significantly lower incidence of heart disease.

LASER

is being used successfully at the **PASADENA FOUNDATION FOR MEDICAL RESEARCH** in the destruction of cancerous tumors.

The operation was a success, but the patient died

A surgical team at the University of Mississippi performs the first heart transplant using the heart from a chimpanzee.

CLEANING OUT THOSE ARTERIES

Representatives of the dairy industry criticize the **American Heart Association** following its recommendation that people reduce the amount of fat they eat and substitute vegetable oils and polyunsaturated fats for animal fats.

Maybe take a break from those coffee breaks?

A naval reserve flight surgeon issues a warning that more than one or two cups of coffee a day could have serious consequences such as heavy heart palpitations that could eventually lead to more serious heart problems.

IS THIS THE START OF SOMETHING GOOD?

New York becomes the 10th state to provide birth control aid to welfare recipients.

According to figures released by the U.S. Public Health Service, the birthrate is declining, probably due in part to the new, more effective oral contraceptives.

"The Pill" has proven 100% effective in preventing pregnancies and might prevent menopause.

An article appearing in the *Journal of the American Medical Association* describes how the birth-control pill Enovid markedly accelerates the growth of existing breast cancers in rats.

Estimated worldwide blind population: 14,000,000

A Brooklyn gynecologist has prevented menopause in 139 women by administering the female hormones, estrogen and progesterone, in controlled doses.

1964

STAY OUT OF THE SMOKING LOUNGE

The Surgeon General condemns cigarette smoking, declaring that smoking contributes substantially to the death rate, primarily by causing lung cancer.

The Special New York State Committee on Smoking & Health denounces cigarette smoking as the cause of "mass murder."

In an effort to stave off federal restrictions, nine U.S. cigarette manufacturers announce the adoption of an advertising code barring cigarette ads from school publications, newspaper comic strips and any other publications directed at persons under 21. Some advertising guidelines:

1. Do not convey the idea that smoking is essential to social prominence, distinction, success or sexual attraction.

2. No testimonials from sports figures or show business personalities.

3. No ads using models engaged in any physical sports.

4. No sponsorship of television shows directed at viewers under 21.

The Federal Trade Commission announces that starting next year, cigarette advertisements and labels will be required to carry a warning "clearly and prominently" stating that cigarette smoking "may cause death from cancer and other diseases."

The AMA puts out a six-page booklet warning that "the longer you smoke and the more you smoke, the greater the risk of developing lung cancer."

San Diego's Naval Hospital reports a higher incidence of natural abortions and premature deliveries among women who smoke.

People who sucked their thumbs when they were infants don't necessarily turn into smokers in their teenage years.

MEANWHILE, BACK AT THE RANCH

The Council for Tobacco Research reports that it finds "little to support" the charge that cigarette smoking caused cancer or "any cardiovascular disease that contributed importantly to mortality."

As a way of controlling the pollution of air in our cities, U.S. cities may be divided into smoking and no smoking zones.

Medical scientists name smog as a factor in the aggravating of heart conditions and respiratory diseases such as asthma, chronic bronchitis, lung cancer, emphysema and common colds.

HOW DO YOU MAKE THE PUNISHMENT FIT THE CRIME?

The Krebiozen Research Foundation of Chicago, and four people who promoted the alleged cancer-arresting drug Krebiozen, are indicted by a federal grand jury on 49 counts of mail fraud, conspiracy, mislabeling and making false statements to the government about the drug.

WATCH THOSE OUTDOOR BARBECUES

Charcoal broiling of meat can produce a chemical compound known to produce cancer in mice, according to two Chicago Medical School researchers.

You've a lot to look for under our sign

More than just an ordinary used car lot.

For one thing, you'll find an extraordinary selection of used Chevies and other makes. From convertibles to pickup trucks. All with plenty of unused miles.

For another, you'll meet an experienced salesman who's also a used car specialist. When you ask questions, he'll give you straight answers—the kind of answers that will help

you make a good choice when you buy.

And, just as if you'd bought a new car, your Chevy dealer's highly trained service staff is there to help you if you ever need it.

So, when you're thinking of buying a good used car or a serviceable truck, remember your Chevrolet dealer's OK sign. It stands for a lot.... Chevrolet Division of General Motors, Detroit, Michigan.

You Can Be What You Are

Researchers at Albert Einstein College of Medicine on heredity vs. environment conclude that while a child is definitely influenced by his or her environment, the child's innate personality characteristics are not strictly dependent on being molded by his or her environment.

Are You Becoming Your Mother?

Research into 50 overweight adolescents from ages 10 to 17 reveals that 35 of the children come from families in which both the mother and father are markedly overweight.

THE NATIONAL INSTITUTION OF HEALTH RELEASES THE FIRST PSYCHIATRIC INVESTIGATION OF LATE ADOLESCENCE AND EARLY ADULTHOOD COURTSHIP.

SOLUTION? RAPID TRANSIT SPACECRAFT

Hughes Aircraft Company scientists discover that the average man driving 60 mph in heavily congested freeways is likely to be more tense than an astronaut cruising in his space capsule.

21,000 people will commit suicide this year.

NO LONGER A SHOCKING EXPERIENCE

The Food & Drug Administration approves Indoklon, a drug that might replace electric shock therapy in treating acute depression.

DR. WILLIAM C. DEMENT, a neurophysiologist at Stanford University's School of Medicine who has made a career of studying sleep, reports that a naturally created toxin from the central nervous system may stimulate dreams.

The Addiction Research Center of the National Institute of Mental Health asserts that evidence suggests that some of the most popular tranquilizers can be addictive and dangerous and can lead to car accidents, accidental setting of fires and violent behavior.

A pamphlet issued by the Public Affairs Committee indicates that tens of thousands of children in America are suffering from serious childhood mental illnesses.

Most headaches are triggered by emotional tension or occupational situations in which the head or neck is held in an awkward or fixed position for long periods of time.

The Journal of the American Medical Association reports the successful use of the synthetic opiate methadone in detoxifying over 20 heroin addicts.

WHAT A YEAR IT WAS!

THIS SAC SHOULD GET THE SACK
Plastic surgeons introduce silicone gel sacs for breast implants.

IS THERE A TRANSPLANT IN *YOUR* FUTURE?
Two out of five Caucasian men will suffer from baldness that usually begins in their late 20s or 30s.

Bursitis accounts for about two-thirds of all shoulder pain, according to a professor of surgery at Columbia University College of Physicians and Surgeons.

THAT OLD ROCKING CHAIR'S GOT HIM
A professor of surgery at Indiana University Medical School sits in his rocking chair between operations, saying that it's extremely rare for a habitual rocker to have swollen feet.

HE'S BUGGING CONGRESS
President Lyndon B. Johnson asks Congress for $29,000,000 to conduct research in safer pest-control methods.

eyes
An artificial cornea that screws into the eye has been developed by Dr. William Stone Jr. of the Massachusetts Eye and Ear Infirmary.

The American Medical Association warns that too many Americans are wearing sunglasses strictly for cosmetic reasons and that in order not to reduce the intensity of their field of vision after sundown, they should definitely not wear them at night.

The Food & Nutrition Board of the National Academy of Sciences National Research Council recommends a daily reduction of 200-300 calories in the average American diet.

Pet dogs of high-cholesterol owners tend to develop the same cholesterol problem as their human masters.

BRACE
YOURSELF FOR THIS ONE
The American Association of Orthodontists holds its 60th annual meeting in Chicago.

MOTOR
IN THE MOUTH
The American Dental Association approves for the first time two electric toothbrushes as effective cleaning devices.

The U.S. Public Health Service reports that 47 million Americans in 2,612 communities are drinking fluoridated water.

1964

NOBEL PRIZES

CHEMISTRY
Dorothy Crowfoot Hodgkin
(U.K.)

PHYSIOLOGY or MEDICINE
Konrad Bloch
(U.S.)

Feodor Lynen
(West Germany)

PHYSICS
Nicolay Gennadiyevich Basov
(U.S.S.R.)

Aleksandr Mikhailovich Prokhorov
(U.S.S.R.)

Charles Hard Townes
(U.S.)

PASSINGS

SCIENCE

RACHEL CARSON, 56
Biologist, author and good friend of the environment, Carson's *The Sea Around Us* broadened the American people's awareness of ecology, was translated into 32 languages and won the National Book Award. Her *Silent Spring* helped alert the nation to the dangers of pesticide use.

LEO SZILARD, 66
Along with Enrico Fermi, Szilard created the first nuclear chain reaction. He fought against the use of nuclear weapons, and received the Atoms for Peace Award.

NORBERT WIENER, 69
Mathematician, scientist, former child prodigy, author, linguist and computer pioneer, he was widely regarded as the father of automation. Wiener also coined the phrase "cybernetics" and received the National Medal of Science.

MEDICINE

DR. ALFRED BLALOCK, 65
Co-developer in 1944 of a heart operation that saves "blue babies."

ANIMAL CORNER

MAYBE YOU'RE A MONKEY'S UNCLE AFTER ALL

Jane Goodall's study of wild chimpanzees in East Africa is expected to call for a revision of opinions about the unique abilities of man.

BETTER CHANGE THAT TUNE

According to a theory developed by Dutch zoologists investigating mass whale strandings, when whales' heads rise out of the water, they cannot screen the echo pings used to avoid collisions, maintain orderly formations and navigate.

PUT AWAY THOSE FISHING RODS & GUNS, GUYS

A Belgian paleontologist heads a group dedicated to preventing the extinction of animals found on the Galapagos Islands since many of the life-forms exist nowhere else in the world.

It is discovered for the first time that cats can see colors.

digging the digs

WHO YOU CALLING A HOMO?

Anthropologist Dr. Louis Leakey reports that he has uncovered fossils in East Africa of a manlike creature who lived one to two million years ago and has named him *Homo habilis*.

THE EARLIEST UNDISTURBED EUROPEAN SITE OF PREHISTORIC STONE TOOLS AND EXTINCT ANIMALS IS DISCOVERED IN HUNGARY.

TRANSLATION: IS IT HOT IN HERE OR IS IT ME?

Excavations in southern Iraq produce clay tablets with cuneiform inscriptions dating back to 4,000 B.C., making them the earliest known written signs.

The Far Eastern Contemporary Model 546 with Stereo FM and AM/FM Radio-Phonograph in Walnut — $795.00

Now Magnavox brings you new dimensions in home entertainment— Magna-Color* with Astro-Sonic** Stereo High Fidelity.

*MAGNA-COLOR—the latest development in color TV—gives brighter pictures in dazzling colors—automatic color tuning that holds colors constant. Quick-ON in seconds. Selective monochrome pictures in beautiful sepia or black and white, as well.

**ASTRO-SONIC Stereo High Fidelity is so revolutionary (no tubes), it is ten times more efficient than the tube sets it obsoletes—flawlessly re-creates the most beautiful music you have ever heard!

And Astro-Sonic gives you high fidelity sound with TV as well as stereo FM/AM radio-phonograph.

Only Magnavox gives you these great features. See the wide variety of elegant styles—in color TV from $449.50, Astro-Sonic consoles from $298.50—at your Magnavox dealer listed in the Yellow Pages.

the magnificent
Magnavox
270 Park Ave., New York 17, N.Y.

The Italian Provincial Model 536 in French Walnut — $595

The Contemporary Astro-Sonic stereo FM and AM/FM radio-phonograph Model 624 — $398.50

BUSINESS 1964

GNP

The Gross National Product is **$625 billion**.

The National Debt, as of June 30, is **$311,713,000,000**.

STOCKS

The Dow Jones passes **800** for the first time. It reaches a record closing high of **891.71**.

18% of American families own stock.

The unemployment rate stays around 5.3%.

%

The Federal Reserve Board raises the prime interest rate from **3-1/2% to 4%**.

Over **9 million** Americans earn less than $3,000.

Over **9 million** working mothers are in the workforce.

TAX

The **federal income tax** cut puts $800 million monthly back into the hands of 74 million working Americans.

California's state tax revenue collections are the highest of any state.

Personal income surpasses $500 billion, a record number.

Per capita income is over $2,300.

LEMONADE

1964
STOCK EXCHANGE

Los Angeles' Times Mirror Co. is the first business that owns an important municipal newspaper to be traded on the New York Stock Exchange.

THE NEW SCOTTISH STOCK EXCHANGE BEGINS TRADING.

Billions are spent on technology and automation, while at the same time jobs are lost to machines.

TEEN FINANCIAL WHIZZES

A half million teenagers own stock.

The average weekly allowance is $4 for girls and $6 for boys.

Teenagers earn approximately $12 billion this year. The girls spend around $450 million on cosmetics while the boys spend 10% of their incomes on dates.

Nearly 15% of teenagers under 20 are unemployed.

SALES SALES & more sales

56% of all baby food sold is made by **Gerber**.

California's **Bullocks, Inc.** and **Federated Department Stores, Inc.** merge.

The **Coca-Cola Co.** merges with **Duncan Foods Co.**

Morton Salt Co. and **Diamond Crystal Salt Co.** are found guilty of price fixing.

Sears, Roebuck & Company opens 17 new stores.

The top 10 retail businesses are:

Sears, Roebuck & Company	Allied Stores
J.C. Penney	May Department Stores
Montgomery Ward	R.H. Macy and Company
Woolworth	Gimbel Brothers
Federated Department Stores	Associated Dry Goods

CAR NEWS

Roughly 7,746,000 cars are made in American car factories.

In December, 870,000 cars roll off U.S. assembly lines, an all-time monthly record.

20% of all autos in the U.S. belong to teenagers.

WHAT A YEAR IT WAS!

STRIKES

1964

THE AVERAGE STRIKE LASTS 25 DAYS.

THE TYPICAL SALARY INCREASE IS 9¢ AN HOUR.

New contracts between the United Automobile Workers and auto companies allow longtime workers with 30 years on the job to retire at 60 with increased benefits.

260,000 members of the United Automobile Workers strike against 89 General Motors Corp. plants for 31 days.

Nine important Ford Motor Co. plants are struck.

Workers strike against the *Detroit Free Press* and *Detroit News* for 134 days. It is the longest strike shutdown against urban daily papers in the history of United States publishing.

A 4 1/2-year-old railroad dispute finally comes to a close with the help of President Johnson. Compromises are made on both sides and wage raises for approximately 100,000 workers cost the railroads about $64 million.

The International Brotherhood of Teamsters signs a country-wide labor agreement with the trucking industry, giving approximately 450,000 workers a 28¢ an hour wage increase plus additional benefits.

The Michigan National Guardsmen arrive in Hillsdale, Michigan to keep order at the Essex Wire Corp. Plant. A strike by the International Union of Electrical Workers turns violent and hundreds of people are on the verge of rioting outside the county jail. Governor George Romney gets involved and helps resolve the conflict.

President Johnson invokes the Taft-Hartley Act against the International Longshoremen's Association to prevent a dock strike. Wildcat strikes begin after the 80-day restraining period imposed by the Act.

EXECUTIVE MOVEMENT

Captain Eddie Rickenbacker
retires as chairman of the board of *Eastern Air Lines*.

Jackie Robinson
becomes chairman of the new *Freedom National Bank*.

Norton Simon
resigns as CEO and president of *Hunt Foods & Industries, Inc.*

John Glenn
becomes a director of *Royal Crown Cola Co.*

Arnold Palmer
becomes chairman of the board of *Arnold Palmer Laundries, Dry Cleaning and Maid Service, Inc.*

WASHKY HERESKY

The first Laundromat opens for business in Moscow.

THE STEEL INDUSTRY
celebrates its 100th anniversary. It all began in Wyandotte, Michigan in September 1864.

Baccarat
celebrates its 200th anniversary with a special exhibit at the Louvre.

WELL, THERE'S LUNCH AT NOON, GOLF AT THREE...
A study reports that many key executives are productive approximately 10% of the time.

PASSINGS

Mark Charles Honeywell, 89
One of the founders and retired chairman of the board of Honeywell Inc.

Ralph Schneider, 55
Co-founder and chairman of the board of Diners Club Inc., the first credit card. The card revolutionized the finance world by allowing people to pay later for merchandise and services.

This Is THE PRICE THAT WAS

FOOD BASKET

Apples (lb.)	.18
Avocados (each)	.19
Bananas (lb.)	.13
Bread (loaf)	.29
Butter (lb.)	.67
Cabbage (lb.)	.05
Cake Mix	.43
Candy Bar	.05
Cereal	.29
Cheddar Cheese (lb.)	.69
Coffee (cup)	.10
Coffee (lb.)	.79
Corn (each)	.05
Cottage Cheese (pt.)	.25
Eggs (dz.)	.37
Grapes (lb.)	.19
Grilled Cheese Sandwich	.45
Honeydew Melon (lb.)	.07
Ice Cream (1/2 gal.)	.59
Mayonnaise	.39
Milk (qt.)	.27
Peanut Butter	.43
Pears (lb.)	.10
Pumpkin Pie	.55
Salad Dressing	.55
Sugar (lb.)	.13
Swiss Cheese (lb.)	.59
TV Dinner	.49
Watermelon (lb.)	.04

YEARLY SALARIES

Stockbroker	$20,000
Doctor	$18,000
Clint Eastwood, "A Fistful of Dollars"	$15,000
Lawyer	$13,000
Editor	$12,000
Computer Programmer	$10,000
Engineer	$8,400
College Professor	$8,200
Nurse, RN	$5,700
Railroad Worker	$7,100
College Graduate, B.A.	$7,000
Construction Worker	$6,700
Teacher	$5,650
Secretary	$4,400
Dictaphone Secretary	$4,100
The Beatles, "The Ed Sullivan Show"	$4,000

HOME SWEET HOME

3-Bedroom House

Carefree, AZ	$100,000
Beverly Hills, CA	$79,500
Newport Beach, CA	$39,500
Great Neck, NY	$37,000
Queens, NY	$29,750
Chicago, IL	$28,900
Glen Rock, NJ	$24,900
Fullerton, CA	$21,950
Rock Lake, WI	$19,000

WHAT A YEAR IT WAS!

THIS OLD HOUSE

Item	Price
4 Life-Size Beatles Pictures	1.98
Aspirin	.89
Bicycle	45.95
Blanket	6.00
Blender	15.88
Clarinet	79.95
Coffeemaker	17.88
Console TV (23")	239.95
Dictionary	4.99
Globe	5.99
Iron	13.66
Laundry Detergent	.79
Lawnmower	99.95
Record (LP)	1.77
Record (45)	.22
Paint (gal.)	2.95
Phonograph w/Radio	59.95
Playpen	10.88
Refrigerator	228.00
Shampoo	1.75
Sheets, Twin	3.98
Stroller	10.88

Item	Price
Tissues	.25
Toothbrush (Automatic)	14.88
Toothpaste	.83
Towel	2.00
Vacuum Cleaner	79.88
Washing Machine	138.00

1964

LA BOUTIQUE

LADIES

Item	Price
Bathing Suit	22.00
Blouse	7.00
Bra	5.00
Chanel No. 5 Cologne	3.50
Designer Evening Dress	190.00
Dress	30.00
Hoop Earrings	5.00
Lipstick	1.25
Mascara	2.00
Nail Polish	.75
Rhinestone Pin	3.00
Pumps	15.00
Scarf	4.25
Shirt	8.00
Sunglasses	13.95

MEN

Item	Price
Belt	3.25
Cologne	5.00
Hat	15.00
Hi-Top Sneakers	6.95
Slacks	14.75
Sport Shirt	3.85
Suit	75.00
Tie	2.50
Watch, Rolex	185.00
Watch, Timex	19.95

STOCKS

Stock	Price	Stock	Price
AT&T	139 1/2	Lane Bryant	29 1/2
Boeing Aircraft	40	Macy's	89 7/8
CBS	43 1/4	Magnavox	29 3/4
Decca Records	45 3/4	MGM	38 3/4
Diners Club	22 3/4	Random House	11 1/8
Eastman Kodak	125	Safeway Stores	69 1/2
General Motors	80 1/4	Sears, Roebuck	124
Gulf & Western	25 1/4	Sheraton	9
Hewlett-Packard	19 1/4	Texaco	84
Holiday Inn	16	US Steel	54 7/8
Kaiser Aluminum	32	Xerox	78 1/2
Kellogg	47 1/2		

1,236,565,422 shares are traded on the New York Stock Exchange.

Are we extravagant for lavishing all these looks on a car all this quick and agile and driveable?

Pontiac Motor Division · General Motors Corporation

Of course not. It's the '65 Pontiac, and we couldn't hide such a quick and nimble car under a what's-that body. So we don't, as you can plainly see. Everything you can't see is new, too, Wide-Track excepted. Our Trophy V-8s breathe deeper now, step off just a little quicker. Then you can specify Turbo Hydra-Matic, the new automatic transmission that shifts smooth as cream but sure as taxes. You're worried the quick new Pontiac won't get along on your budget? Don't fret. Our economy rear axle gobbles up so much highway on a tank of gas, you'll wish your credit card were good at toll booths. Try a '65 at your Pontiac dealer.

Pontiac for 1965
The year of the Quick Wide-Tracks

DISASTERS

Domestic Diasters

OVER 100,000 PEOPLE DIE IN VARIOUS TYPES OF ACCIDENTS.

Of the nearly 48,000 killed in automobile accidents, 504 die over the July 4th holiday while 531 perish over the Labor Day weekend.

An airline passenger shoots the pilot and co-pilot, forcing a plane en route to San Francisco from Reno to crash into a mountain. All 44 people on board are killed.

140 people die on the East Coast during a four-day storm that brings freezing temperatures.

Melting snow, broken dams and an overflowing river set off major flooding in Montana, killing 30 and causing $70 million in property damage.

Rains and floods in California, Oregon, Washington, Nevada and Idaho kill over 40, leave thousands homeless and result in roughly $1 billion in damage.

Hurricane Hilda generates two separate tornadoes, causing $100 million in damage and killing 36 people in Louisiana.

The Alaskan Earthquake Aftermath

A TIDAL WAVE caused by the Alaskan earthquake kills over a dozen people in Crescent City, California. Streets in Houston, Texas rise up approximately five inches. Tsunamis reach Japan and Siberia.

South Of The Border

In **Lima, Peru**, over 300 soccer fans are killed, and hundreds more injured, during a riot that takes place when fans disagree with a referee's call during a championship Peru-Argentina game.

1964

ALASKA IS SHAKEN BY THE GREATEST EARTHQUAKE EVER RECORDED ON THE NORTH AMERICAN CONTINENT

Great crevices open in the earth and literally swallow everything.

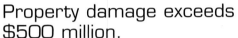

Property damage exceeds $500 million.

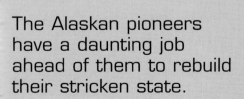

The Alaskan pioneers have a daunting job ahead of them to rebuild their stricken state.

WHAT A YEAR IT WAS!

PUT A TIGER IN <u>YOUR</u> TANK!

"BUT GEORGE...
I'M SURE
I HEARD A ROAR"

Check local listing for time and date.
Watch for the Enco Report on NBC-TV.

NEW POWER-FORMULA ENCO EXTRA GASOLINE BOOSTS POWER THREE WAYS:

1 Cleaning Power! Dirt can clog even a new carburetor in a few months of normal operation—causing hard starting and rough idling. Your very first tankful of New Enco Extra will start to clear away these deposits—in new engines or old—to improve power and mileage.

2 Firing Power! Spark plug and cylinder deposits can cause misfiring, pre-ignition and hot spots. New Enco Extra neutralizes these harmful deposits—to help your engine fire smoothly, to help preserve the power of new cars and restore lost power to many older cars.

3 Octane Power! New Enco Extra has the high octane that most cars now need for full smooth performance without knocking.

You'll get *all* these extras with New Power-formula Enco Extra gasoline — it puts a tiger in your tank! *Happy Motoring!*

HUMBLE
OIL & REFINING COMPANY

MAKERS OF FINE ENCO PRODUCTS
AND THE ENCO RACING FUELS THAT
POWERED A. J. FOYT AND RODGER

WARD TO FIRST AND SECOND PLACE
IN THIS YEAR'S INDIANAPOLIS 500
MEMORIAL DAY CLASSIC

153

The second best shape in Italy

at the hottest little price in the USA. You've seen the first, in films. Now see the Fiat, in person. Fiat is the hot one. The Italians did it the way they do most things. With style. With flair. With flourish. And there's no Germanic thrift showing. This Fiat sport comes with all the extras at not a penny extra. Bucket seats, power brakes, leatherette upholstery, heater, defroster, tachometer, dual electric wipers, safety belt anchors, bumper guards, self-cancelling turn signals, help-lights and tool kit. And speaking of figures, you can't even come close to a shape like this at a price so trim and appealing. At **FIAT** $2639*, it's the lowest-priced sports car in its class. Every family should have at least one Fiat.

*Suggested prices, p.o.e., New York. Sales and service throughout U.S. and Canada. For overseas delivery see your Fiat Dealer, travel agent, or write Fiat Motor Company, Inc., 500 Fifth Ave., New York 36, N.

SPORTS 1964

Storybook Finish For The St. Louis Cardinals

THE CARDINALS *meet the* **NEW YORK YANKEES** *in New York for the World Series championship.*

It's the fourth inning of the final game and **Tim McCarver** swings and bounces to second.

The throw to first base is wild.

CONTINUES...

WHAT A YEAR IT WAS!

155

Storybook Finish For The
St. Louis Cardinals

McCarver is safe at first (*left*) and **Ken Boyer** scores the first Cardinal run (*right*).

Mel Stottlemyre pitches to **Dal Maxvill** (*above*), and the Cards pull a double steal (*left, top inset*) that sends McCarver to third (*left*).

When Maxvill singles home a third run, the Cards go ahead in this fourth inning and there they stay until they are crowned World Champs in the ninth.

St. Louis beats the Yankees 4-3, winning their first World Series since 1946.

BASEBALL ● NEWS

WORLD SERIES

St. Louis Cardinals over New York Yankees, 4-3

⚾ Los Angeles Dodgers pitcher **Johnny Podres**, 31, is out of commission for at least a month following surgery to remove a bone fragment from his pitching elbow.

⚾ St. Louis Cardinal **Stan "The Man" Musial** is at home recovering after his collapse from exhaustion at a Cardinals-Braves game brought on by his responsibilities as the nation's physical fitness director.

⚾ The Yankees fire **Mel Allen**, longtime television and radio voice, who popularized the "going, going, gone" home run call and often said "how about that" to describe happenings on the ball field.

⚾ **Ken Johnson** is the first pitcher to throw a nine-inning no-hitter and lose.

⚾ **Jim Bunning** of the Philadelphia Phillies pitches the National League's first perfect game in 84 years.

⚾ Los Angeles Dodger **Sandy Koufax** pitches his third no-hitter.

⚾ New York Mets manager **Casey Stengel** celebrates his 74th birthday.

⚾ The National League sets a new major-league attendance record of 12,045,193 for the 1964 season.

⚾ Giants catcher **Joe Garagiola**, 38, announces his voluntary retirement from baseball to become a radio and television broadcaster in St. Louis.

Shea Stadium, the Mets' new home replacing the Polo Grounds, is christened with the Dodgers' holy water from the Gowanus Canal in Brooklyn and the Giants' holy water from the Harlem River.

The San Francisco Giants beat the New York Mets 8-6 in a 23-inning game that runs 7 hours, 23 minutes.

BASEBALL BUSINESS

CBS becomes the first corporate owner of a major-league team, buying 80% of the Yankees for $11,200,000.

Philadelphia voters approve $25 million to build a new sport stadium.

Lefty **Warren Spahn** of the Milwaukee Braves signs an $85,000 contract, making him the highest-paid pitcher in baseball history.

32-year-old Giants outfielder **Willie Mays** signs a $105,000 contract, making him the highest-paid player in baseball.

Baseball executives vote to hold a free-agent draft in New York City.

ABOUT YOGI

Despite a 99-63 record, the Yankees fire manager Yogi Berra after losing the World Series to the Cardinals.

The Mets sign Yogi Berra to a two-year contract to coach under his old Yankees boss, Casey Stengel.

Three days after resigning as manager of the world champion Cardinals, Johnny Keane replaces Yogi Berra as the Yankees' field boss.

CY YOUNG AWARD

DEAN CHANCE, LA

Home Run Leaders

National League
Willie Mays (SF, 47)

American League
Harmon Killebrew (Minnesota, 49)

Batting Champions

National League
Roberto Clemente (Pittsburgh, .339)

American League
Tony Oliva (Minnesota, .323)

Most Valuable Player

National League
Ken Boyer (St. Louis)

American League
Brooks Robinson (Baltimore)

Strikeouts

National League
Bob Veale (Pittsburgh, 250)

American League
Al Downing (NY, 217)

Stolen Bases

National League
Maury Wills (LA, 53)
(5 years in a row)

American League
Luis Aparicio (Baltimore, 57)
(9 years in a row)

All-Star Game

National over American, 7-4

1964 NBA CHAMPION

THE BOSTON CELTICS get an early jump as they battle the **SAN FRANCISCO WARRIORS** for the NBA championship. The Celtics are after their sixth crown in a row.

Fans are dressed in their Sunday finest.

Boston's **SAM JONES** is in rare form.

JOHN HAVLICEK loops it in.

WILT CHAMBERLAIN, number 13, is the leading scorer for the Warriors with 30 points

Celtic star **K.C. JONES** shoots and misses.

THE WARRIORS take the ball.

K.C. JONES steals the ball to score.

In the final quarter the **CELTICS** slowly pull ahead after trailing momentarily.

WHAT A YEAR IT WAS!

SHIP

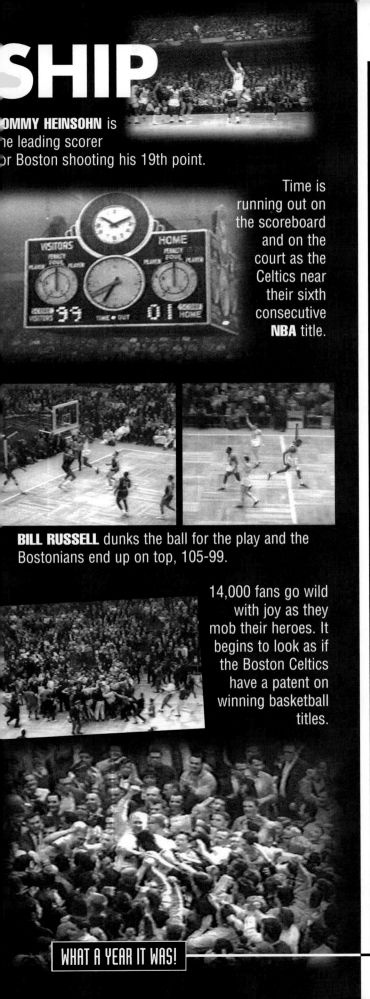

TOMMY HEINSOHN is the leading scorer for Boston shooting his 19th point.

Time is running out on the scoreboard and on the court as the Celtics near their sixth consecutive **NBA** title.

BILL RUSSELL dunks the ball for the play and the Bostonians end up on top, 105-99.

14,000 fans go wild with joy as they mob their heroes. It begins to look as if the Boston Celtics have a patent on winning basketball titles.

WHAT A YEAR IT WAS!

What's The Latest Hoop-La

Princeton basketball star **BILL BRADLEY**, the nation's highest scorer in major college competition with 939 points, turns down a chance to turn pro to attend Oxford as a Rhodes scholar, saying that athletes "retire at 30 with nothing more than a scrapbook of their clippings."

The NCAA penalizes four colleges for excessive financial aid to their athletes and their recruiting practices: Michigan State, Miami, Navy and Western State College.

With their sixth consecutive championship, the Boston Celtics are rated tops of any sports team.

DOLPH SCHAYES, the greatest Jewish player in NBA history and first NBA player to score 15,000 points, retires this year with 19,249 points.

GO BRUINS!

UCLA is undefeated this season, a feat accomplished only twice before by San Francisco in 1956 and North Carolina in 1957.

For the first time in his career, **WILT CHAMBERLAIN** either leads or is among the leaders in all three major categories—scoring, rebounds and assists.

NBA president **WALTER KENNEDY** negotiates a five-year contract with ABC to broadcast a game of the week.

NBA STATISTICS

CHAMPIONS
Boston Celtics over San Francisco Warriors 4-1 (sixth consecutive win)

SCORING LEADER SEASON
Wilt Chamberlain San Francisco Warriors 36.9 avg.

REBOUNDS SEASON
Bill Russell Boston 24.7 avg.

FREE THROWS PERCENTAGE
Oscar Robertson Cincinnati .853

ASSISTS
Oscar Robertson Cincinnati 868

MOST VALUABLE PLAYER
Oscar Robertson Cincinnati

ROOKIE OF THE YEAR
Jerry Lucas Cincinnati

FIELD GOALS PERCENTAGE
Jerry Lucas Cincinnati .527

NBA ALL-STAR GAME
East over West 111-107

NCAA CHAMPIONS
UCLA over Duke 98-83

COACH OF THE YEAR
UCLA John Wooden

STANDARD OIL COMPANY OF CALIFORNIA (METHYL®)

This weekend, while you mow

and tow,

hose

and doze (ha!),

shop

and drop...

we'll check things through,

freshen your view,

keep you going like new!

Take time out at the sign of the Chevron for service as friendly as it is thorough. Then get a powerful new start with one of our three Chevron gasolines.

Why do we have three? The answer lies in the different power requirements of today's automobile engines.

Super-powered cars go best with *Custom*— highest-quality gasoline in the West. Other high-compression cars get peak performance with *Supreme*. Cars that run on regular get all the power they can deliver with *Chevron*. The point is, you pay only for your car's needs, not the other fellow's.

And in the bargain, you get Methyl, the different antiknock compound that helps bring out all the power built into your car. *Why not come in and get going?*

At the sign of the Chevron

Chevron Dealers · Standard Stations

We take better care of your car

160

FOOTBALL 1964

NATIONAL FOOTBALL LEAGUE CHAMPIONS
Cleveland Browns over
Baltimore Colts
27-0

NFL MOST VALUABLE PLAYER
Johnny Unitas
(Baltimore)

AMERICAN FOOTBALL LEAGUE CHAMPIONS
Buffalo Bills over
San Diego Chargers
20-7

NATIONAL COLLEGE FOOTBALL CHAMPIONS
Alabama, 10-1-0
(AP, UPI)
Arkansas, 11-0-0
(FWAA)
Notre Dame, 9-1-0
(NFF)

ROSE BOWL
Illinois over
Washington
17-7

HEISMAN TROPHY
John Huarte
Notre Dame
Quarterback

NFL NUMBER ONE DRAFT CHOICE
Dave Parks, End
Texas Tech to
San Francisco 49ers

NFL PRO BOWL
West over East
31-17

PIGSKIN NEWS

BRIAN PICCOLO at Wake Forest leads the NCAA Division I-A in scoring with 17 touchdowns and 111 points.

BETTER SELL A LOT OF BEER, BOYS
In the highest price ever paid for broadcast rights, the NFL awards its 1964-65 championship game rights to CBS for $1.8 million per game.

With a salary of $60,000 a year, Cleveland Browns fullback 28-year-old **JIMMY BROWN** is football's highest-paid player.

23 million fans,
a record number, attend
college games this year.

The AFL sets a new single-game attendance record when 60,300 people show up for the Buffalo Bills vs. New York Jets game in New York City.

The 30th Annual Masters Golf Tournament

FANS ARE HERE FOR WHAT SHOULD BE A MOST EXCITING EVENT.

Jack Nicklaus comes down to the final hole with the lowest score for the day and winds up with a 282 (*top left*), six under par as he misses this birdie three (*bottom left*).

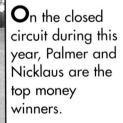

This is the 20-foot birdie that gives Arnold Palmer a grand total that is 12 strokes under par.

On the closed circuit during this year, Palmer and Nicklaus are the top money winners.

This victory pulls Palmer out of a six-month slump and he wears the robe of a new king—the traditional Masters jacket.

golf STATISTICS

1964

U.S. OPEN	Ken Venturi Mickey Wright (4th time)
PGA/LPGA	Bobby Nichols Mary Mills
PGA/LPGA LEADING MONEY WINNER	Jack Nicklaus $113,284.50 Mickey Wright $29,800
PGA PLAYER OF THE YEAR	Ken Venturi
MASTERS	Arnold Palmer
U.S. AMATEUR	Bill Campbell Barbara McIntire
BRITISH OPEN	Tony Lema
SENIOR PGA	Sam Snead

GOLF NOTES

Officially out of his slump after losing 11 straight tournaments, Arnold Palmer wins an unprecedented fourth Masters title with a $20,000 purse as well as the Piccadilly Match Play title in England.

SPARRING NEWS

HEAVYWEIGHT
CASSIUS CLAY (MUHAMMAD ALI) beats **Sonny Liston** who is a 7-1 favorite.

LIGHT HEAVYWEIGHT
WILLIE PASTRANO

MIDDLEWEIGHT
JOEY GIARDELLO

WELTERWEIGHT
EMILE GRIFFITH

LIGHTWEIGHT
CARLOS ORTIZ

FEATHERWEIGHT
ULTIMINIO "Sugar" RAMOS

VICENTE SALDIVAR

"THE RING" MAGAZINE FIGHT OF THE YEAR
Cassius Clay over **Sonny Liston** KO 7

Three days before **Cassius Clay** is set to fight **Sonny Liston**, Clay is rushed to City Hospital where surgery is performed on a hernia.

Cassius Clay

HO, HO, HO, WHO'S GOT THE LAST LAUGH NOW?
The Army makes its official ruling that Cassius Clay, aka Muhammad Ali, is not intelligent enough to be drafted.

Ex-heavyweight boxing champion **Joe Louis** turns 50 and celebrates with a birthday party on the 50th floor of Manhattan's Americana Hotel.

Ex-world welterweight boxing champion **Kid Gavilan** is serving a five-year prison term in Havana.

Nine professional and five amateur fighters die from boxing injuries this year, with only one death in American boxing.

HOCKEY

STANLEY CUP CHAMPIONS

TORONTO MAPLE LEAFS
over
DETROIT RED WINGS
4-3 (third year)

ROSS TROPHY
(LEADING SCORER)

STAN MIKITA (Chicago)

VEZINA TROPHY
(OUTSTANDING GOALIE)

CHARLIE HODGE (Montreal)

CALDER MEMORIAL TROPHY
(ROOKIE OF THE YEAR)

JACQUES LAPERRIERE (Montreal)

LADY BYNG MEMORIAL TROPHY
(MOST GENTLEMANLY PLAYER)

KEN WHARRAM (Chicago)

HART MEMORIAL TROPHY (MVP)

JEAN BELIVEAU
(Montreal)

Hockey News

Gordie Howe of the
Detroit Red Wings
scores his 627th goal,
an NHL record.

WHAT A YEAR IT WAS!

TRAGEDY STRIKES THE 48TH RUNNING OF THE INDIANAPOLIS SPEEDWAY FAMED 500

33 cars start in this classic with tragedy behind the wheel from the start.

As they come into the straightaway on the second lap, **Dave McDonald** loses control of his Juggernaut and spins into the wall.

It starts a chain reaction as seven other cars pile up.

Blinded by smoke and flames, **Eddie Sachs** smashes into McDonald and is killed. McDonald dies later in the hospital. **Ronnie Duman** scrambles over the infield wall badly burned but alive.

The race is halted for one hour and 45 minutes to clear the track.

The first driver across the finish line is **A.J. Foyt**, with an average speed of 147 mph, a new record time.

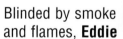

WHAT A YEAR IT WAS!

CAR RACING

INDIANAPOLIS 500

A.J. Foyt
Sheraton-Thompson Special,
147.350 mph

LE MANS

Jean Guichet & Nino Vaccarella
Ferrari 275, 121.54 mph

WINSTON CUP

Richard Petty

WOMEN'S WORLD LAND SPEED RECORD

Paula Murphy
226.37 mph

LAND SPEED RECORD

Art Arfons
536.71 mph

(He breaks **Craig Breedlove**'s record of 526.28 mph.)

FLYING A DIFFERENT HIGH WITH THE ROYAL FORCE

The RAF doesn't do all of its flying in planes. This is their physical training display team that is limbering up for the Royal Tournament.

Some have never done this stunting until a few weeks ago, but now look at them (*top left*), especially on the trampoline (*right*)!

Their marvelous sense of timing came only with practice.

There's no doubt that these are flyboys and when they unveil this act at Earl's Court during the Royal Tournament, they're sure to be a hit of the show. They might even have the audience jumping for joy!

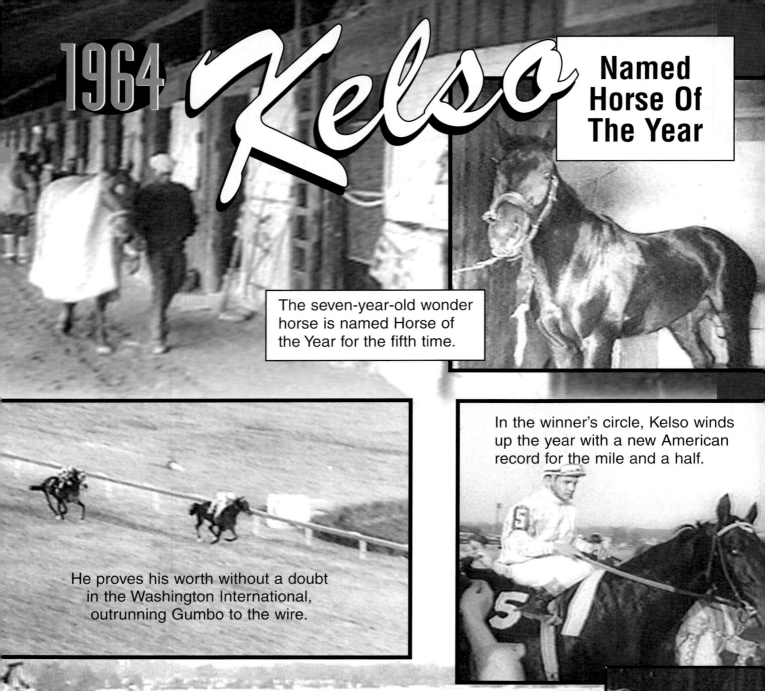

1964

Kelso

Named Horse Of The Year

The seven-year-old wonder horse is named Horse of the Year for the fifth time.

He proves his worth without a doubt in the Washington International, outrunning Gumbo to the wire.

In the winner's circle, Kelso winds up the year with a new American record for the mile and a half.

WHAT A YEAR IT WAS!

HORSE RACING

KENTUCKY DERBY

Northern Dancer, *ridden by* **Bill Hartack**

PREAKNESS STAKES

Northern Dancer, *ridden by* **Bill Hartack**

BELMONT STAKES

Quadrangle, *ridden by* **Manuel Ycaza**

HORSE OF THE YEAR

Kelso

(5TH YEAR IN A ROW)

MONEY LEADERS

Jockey **Willie Shoemaker***
$2,649,553
(7TH YEAR IN A ROW)

Horse **Gun Bow**
$580,100

*Atop **Slapstick**, "The Shoe" rides to his 5,000th victory, putting him into second place in all-time victories.

Rated as one of the greatest horses of all time, Kelso retires with record earnings of more than $1,800,000.

WHAT A YEAR IT WAS!

1964

Figure Skating

World Champions

- **Manfred Schnelldorfer** (West Germany)
- **Sjoukje Dijkstra** (Holland)

U.S. Champions

- **Scott Allen**
- **Peggy Fleming**

Canadian National

- **Charles Snelling**
- **Petra Burka**

RODEO

ALL-AROUND
CHAMPION
COWBOY

DEAN OLIVER

1964 OLYMPIC

The U.S. does very well in the international games and one of Uncle Sam's outstanding heroes is an 18-year-old swimmer, Don Schollander.

At the national gymnasium, the Tokyo audience is riveted by young Don's performance in the 100-meter freestyle as he sets a new Olympic record.

The highlight is the 100-mete streaking dow

Bob wins the race in 10 seconds flat and adds another gold medal to Uncle Sam's bag.

A thrilled fan.

Swimming in lane five, Schollander goes the distance in 53.4 seconds.

The youngster receives another of the four medals he wins for the U.S.

SAYON

WHAT A YEAR IT WAS!

GAMES — 1964

e track events
ith Bob Hayes
the far lane.

SUMMER OLYMPICS TOKYO
(FIRST OLYMPICS HELD IN ASIA)

COUNTRY	# GOLD MEDALS
USA	36
USSR	30
JAPAN	16
GERMANY	10
BRITAIN	4

TOTAL MEDALS	
USSR	96
USA	90

800 METERS & 1,500 METERS
Peter Snell
New Zealand

100-METER DASH
Bob Hayes
USA

HEAVYWEIGHT BOXING CHAMPION
Joe Frazier, USA

The U.S. basketball team maintains a perfect U.S. Olympic record, winning nine games and losing none.

WINTER OLYMPICS INNSBRUCK

500-METER RACE, SPEED SKATING
Terry McDermott, 23
(In the biggest upset of the games, **McDermott** beats the world's greatest skater, USSR's **Yevgeny Grishin**.)

In the Winter Olympics, the U.S.S.R. leads all other nations by a wide margin, winning a total of 25 medals including 11 gold.

t's time
to say
ayonara
another
ur years
l Mexico
in 1968.

As a side note, due to its apartheid policy, South Africa is barred from the Tokyo Olympics.

TRACK & FIELD

BOSTON MARATHON
Aurele Vandendriessche
Belgium

POLE VAULT
Fred Hansen
17 feet, 1 inch
(new world record)

1964

CHESS

WORLD CHAMPION

Tigran Petrosian (U.S.S.R.)

U.S. CHAMPION

Bobby Fisher • Sonja Graf

CYCLING

TOUR de FRANCE

Jacques Anquetil
France
(4TH IN A ROW)

INTERNATIONAL YO-YO CONTEST

PATRICK MALEY
RETURN TOP

PETER SPAN
SPIN TOP

TENNIS

U.S. OPEN

ROY EMERSON over **FRED STOLLE**

MARIA BUENO over **CAROLE GRAEBNER**

WIMBLEDON*

ROY EMERSON over **FRED STOLLE**

MARIA BUENO over **MARGARET SMITH**

DAVIS CUP

AUSTRALIA over **USA, 3-2**

*Emerson and Bueno repeat their Wimbledon wins with victories at Forest Hills.

AMERICA'S CUP

USA
Constellation
outsails **Sovereign**
(Britain)

PASSINGS

Walter Brown, 59
President of the Boston Garden and co-owner of the Boston Celtics basketball team and Boston Bruins hockey team.

Art Ross, 78
National Hockey League Hall of Famer, coach of the first American professional hockey team, the Boston Bruins, and inspiration for the Art Ross Trophy, given annually to the NHL player who leads in scoring.

WHAT A YEAR IT WAS!

DOG SHOW WINNER

WESTMINSTER KENNEL CLUB

Best in Show
Courtenay Fleetfoot
of Pennyworth

Whippet (1st Whippet to Win Best in Show)

CAT OF THE YEAR
Shawnee Moonflight

Persian

POCKET BILLIARDS

Luther Lassiter
2ND CONSECUTIVE
WORLD CHAMPIONSHIP

BOWLING

BPAA ALL-STAR TOURNAMENT — **BOB STRAMPE** / **LaVERNE CARTER**

BPA / WPBA — **BOB STRAMPE** / **BETTY KUCZYNSKI**

BOWLER OF THE YEAR — **BILLY HARDWICK** / **LaVERNE CARTER**

ASSORTED AWARDS

AP ATHLETE OF THE YEAR
Don Schollander (Swimming)
Mickey Wright (Golf)

SPORTS ILLUSTRATED SPORTSMAN OF THE YEAR
Ken Venturi
GOLF

JAMES E. SULLIVAN MEMORIAL AWARD
Don Schollander
(Swimming)

BEST ALL-AROUND SURFER
Mark Martinson

THE HICKOK BELT
Jim Brown
(Football)

FISHING

Peter Simons
149-pound
amberjack (Bermuda)

B.C. Bain
415-pound striped marlin
(Cape Brett, New Zealand)

FAMOUS BIRTHS

Bonnie **BLAIR**

Dwight **GOODEN**

Barry **BONDS**

Ron **HARPER**

Jose **CANSECO**

Brett **HULL**

1964 WAS A GREAT YEAR, BUT...

THE BEST IS YET TO COME!